My <u>LoveDance</u>®

I0198173

A Memoir

Deborah Maragopoulos FNP,

The Hormone Queen®

Intuitive Integrative Family Nurse Practitioner

shares lessons learned as spirit on a human journey.

Published by Genesis Health Products, Inc. Printed in the United States of America.

ISBN-10: 1940112028   ISBN-13: 978-1940112022

This publication is designed to provide accurate and authoritative information with regard to the subject matter covered. It is sold with the understanding that the publisher is not engaged in rendering legal, accounting, or other professional advice. If legal advice or other expert assistance is required, the services of a competent professional should be sought.

Most Genesis Health Products titles are available at special quantity discounts for bulk purchases for sales promotions, premiums, fundraising, and educational use. Special versions or book excerpts can also be created to fit specific needs. For more information, please write-in, or visit:

Genesis Health Products, Inc. 222 Sierra Rd Ojai, CA 93023
www.Genesis-Health-Products.com
(805) 640-3341

For Steve, who lovingly partnered with me in my most precious

<u>LoveDance</u>®

ACKNOWLEDGEMENTS

I want to express my appreciation for everyone who inspired me to write this book. My patients and friends who encouraged me to unveil my journey. My children Jarys and Kyra who expect me to be my most authentic self. Gaby, my amazing assistant, who helps me heal others with grace. My son-in-law Thomas who helped me in the publishing process. And most of all, my beloved husband Steve who has always supported me emotionally, physically, and spiritually through every transformation. Thank you, dear ones, I couldn't have done it without you!

INTRODUCTION

After reading my 50th birthday post on Facebook, a friend from elementary school came to see me as a patient. As if we were never separated...our friendship re-bloomed after 25 years apart. Then she read my book — LoveDance® — and asked, "When did you begin your spiritual journey?"

I answered: When I realized I am spirit on a human journey.

I am living my dream. I feel it before it happens. I celebrate this grand adventure. I am living life in sacred relationship with my beloved husband of 33 years, with my enlightened children and their spouses, with my very human family who loves me in spite of my transformation, with my patients who come more and more ripe to receive healing, with my circle of friends who each dance beautifully with me in their uniquely loving ways.

Like most, I began my adult life playing the game of being human — I became a Human Doing. We are so good at Doing, yet not so good at Being. We judge ourselves by what we've accomplished, what we've done. One of my greatest life lessons has been to become a Human Being. I did this by remembering that I am not a human on a spiritual journey. I am spirit on a human journey.

I've always known. Yet the world around me didn't seem ready to remember. Most of my life, I felt different than my sisters, my peers, my colleagues. I felt out of tune with them. I was dancing to a different beat. It wasn't until I danced among other spiritual seekers that I realized my rhythm.

Yet I had little in common with the spiritual seekers. Most were seeking to ascend the human condition. Few lived in intimate relationships with others. I believe enlightenment is found in our human relationships. And so many spiritual seekers suffered in their human form. I don't believe suffering is our innate human condition.

I believe in fully investing in this life here on earth. Allowing spirit to lead. Releasing mental constructs that no longer serve. Perceiving life through new senses. Feeling my emotions. Learning my soul lessons. Becoming more refined vibrationally. Upregulating my DNA so that I might enjoy the journey in physical form as I hold more light.

I don't have a way to show you. I have my story. How I got to where I am—spiritually, mentally, and physically. My way of ascending. Perhaps it's yours too. Perhaps in reading my story, you might remember who you are, why you are here, and where we are going. Thanks to my curious friend, I know the time is ripe to share my story.

I've been writing since I was a teenager. Stories, novelettes, poetry and, of course, a diary. I even wrote letters to God. I did a bit of professional writing, published in health care journals, but it wasn't until I wrote my first novel—<u>LoveDance</u>®: <u>Awakening the Divine Daughter</u>—did I find story telling to be the best way to teach. I share my stories when I consult with patients, when I lecture to audiences both professional and public, and when I am in circle with my women friends. Story is how we learn.

In this book, I am including writings from my past so you can see where I've come from. All of it is my truth as I understood it at the time.

While I hope my writing is enlightening, in essence this is my healing journey. I have kept a journal since my youth. The pages have always welcomed me, comforted me in times of sorrow, and gave me space to place my reflections. In writing, I learn more about me, about my life, about my world. And usually it is what I cared most to record in my precious journal that I use to comfort others.

A memoir lays you wide open and quite bare…yet it is who I am…like the heroine of my first book—Mary Magdalen—I unveil my heart and soul easily.

My first book <u>LoveDance</u>® is a novel. I started with fiction because I was afraid to tell my story. So I told HerStory and remembered the Sacred Feminine Way of Healing. I had been practicing it, in the guise of Intuitive Integrative Medicine, yet now I was living it, embodying the Sacred Feminine and finally felt whole.

And my healing practice which focused on treating the Hormonally Challenged expanded. I began openly treating the whole person. Body, Mind and Soul. As I began embodying my own <u>LoveDance</u>®, I began to teach what I knew, really knew in my heart, in my soul, in every cell of my body…I knew how to heal. I knew how to be in relationship with men, women and children. I remembered how to dance with the Earth herself…my DNA was dancing health.

My husband, a retired police officer, says that taking an accident report from three witnesses reveals three different stories. Everyone has their unique perspective. Each of my family members has theirs. And I have mine. This is not their story. It is mine from my unique perspective.

My mother read my story ten years ago and didn't agree. So I went deeper and left out what I assumed was her perspective and just presented mine. After reading this version of my story, she nodded, "Finally you're telling your story, not mine."

I am no longer hiding behind anyone else's veil. I am ready to unveil my soul to you, my reader. Those in my story may not be ready to unveil theirs. So they are clothed by alias names. My mother was proud to be named by her given name...so she is who she is.

She may have cast the veil from her face, but I am utterly naked. It is my nature to unveil my all to know myself more deeply, to share my experiences and what I have learned in being in human form on this beautiful earth.

I turned 55 on the Spring Equinox 2016. I have always known that the old me would not exist at this time. I am transforming. And now I share my journey with you, finally.

Love & Light,

Deborah

Table of Contents

Part One
CHOOSING LOVE

I enter the cave from the cove. Bright orange fish reflect the fading light. Swimming silently in the brisk dark water, I go deeper. Voices echo indistinctly as kayakers enter the ocean side of this long dark sea cavern. The tunnel curves so the light cannot follow. I can see nothing. Only feel the brush of kelp against my bare legs and smooth fluttering of fish passing near. I raise my masked face to take in the dark. This could be scary if I chose fear. But I choose love. And swim on through the dark.

My niece swims past me never raising her head, so I follow her out to the open ocean. I promised her mother, I would watch over her. We wait for my sister to join us. We wait and wait. And after a long while, my sister appears. She clutches a rock nearest the tunnel and rips off her mask, breathing hard, panic emanating from her. She looked up in the dark and chose fear.

I calm her down. Get her to use my snorkel to slow her breath…and swim with one hand on her back. My sister blames her reaction on a kayaker taking underwater photography. "It was creepy. Pornographic!" I sigh…we are in wetsuits. When choosing fear…we often need to find something to be afraid of. I asked my niece if she was frightened. "No, you were with me."

Three ways of being human. We can be like a little child and Trust. We can be like most of humanity and reflexively choose Fear. Or we can be conscious and choose Love.

Always three choices. The world is not duality, but a trinity of possibility.

This life I chose Love.

2. ALL IS OF THE DIVINE

August 6th, 1983

I married my beloved. We were sealed together for all eternity. We took it seriously…the sealing…although I have a certain amnesia when it comes to the secret temple ceremony. Sort of like Mary. My life is loosely portrayed in Mary's story. I called it LoveDance®: Awakening the Divine Daughter … but it is My LoveDance®…my Awakening to my Divine Daughter Potential…and with that I became whole…fully embodying the

Divine Mother and now becoming the Crone (the Divine Grandmother energy of the Triple Goddess).

I have a memory of being in my mother's womb, looking between my legs to find NOTHING…and feeling great despair because I knew how hard it would be to accomplish my mission on earth in female form. Thank the goddess, the world shifted during my lifetime…or did I shift my world?

I have started writing my story so many times. I have lots of stories collected over the years…my experiences as a human being. I have read with interest other's stories of their awakening to their power…especially women…who tend to be more intimate in their story telling. Mine is different, I believe, in that I came knowing this life was about joy. I remember a calm acceptance of the family I chose… a gentle leading of my mother and father as I taught them how to parent me. A shepherding of my sisters…protecting and guiding them. Then a great need to be me…yet perceiving the world as unsupportive…I arrested my blossoming womanhood until I met my beloved.

I do not remember a time when I was not in communication with the earth, with the animals, with the plants. I have always felt others…their hopes, their fears, their dis-ease…I sometimes heard their thoughts, but mostly knew their hearts…their truth…saw their divine light. I learned very early the system of being human. How not to get distracted by the unseen in order to be present in reality. It's as if I have been able to maintain my 3D channel while simultaneously watching many other channels…some I gathered information from, some entertained me, some guided me.

The past and the future were intertwined with my present. I could always see my future, dreaming of it many years before it would come to pass. I learned very early to wrinkle time…I remember reading A Wrinkle in Time and knowing that the author knew how too. I also remember disappearing.

I slipped in and out of the reality in which my friends and family existed quite easily. Playing hide and seek, I used this ability. I did not think of it as a talent then, I just did it. Only in writing Mary's story did I consider how I did it. Before Mary's story came to me, I did not consider my past lives.

Well, I did have a dream just before dreaming I was Mary Magdalen. *I was a gypsy in a concentration camp. My husband had been killed. My daughter had been safely removed from the country by my father. I was a healer and the Nazis were using my abilities to assist in their experiments. I found a way to thwart them by releasing the souls of their victims before they could finish torturing them. I worked with my deceased spouse (the same one I'm married to now) who would take their souls through the veil. I knew they would eventually kill me, but I was not frightened…rather excited by our subterfuge.* I woke up in joyous wonder of that time.

I knew then as I know now that all is of the Divine. Yes, all…the good, the bad and the ugly. It's a matter of perspective. It's our choice how we perceive life's events. We can choose fear as the container to hold our experiences. Or we can choose love.

3. SNAKE MEDICINE

On a hot summer morning, my last day of vacation before work resumes, I am searching for something on the back of my horse. Shane has a hesitant energy about her, barn-sour perhaps, missing her goat. I ask her to move on, but she stops three times on the trail. Charlie, my border collie-greyhound mix tucks himself under her tail. Both are usually gregarious, anxious to get out, to run side by side. Not today.

I reminisce. Our vacation in Cancun last week was amazing. A heart felt sensuous discovery. Kundalini energy rising from the alabaster sand through the turquoise sea and into puffy white clouds floating in the azure sky. Serpentine spirals floating in my heart chakra. I see these same serpentine energies — a dance of silver and gold — arising from my pituitary into my crown, down my spine and into my mare's. Her hooves solidify our connection to the earth.

At the crest of the trail, the watering hole is dry. I dismount at the fire gate and water the dog. My mare is anxious, and Charlie drinks little attending only to her. As I mount up, Shane moves out from under me. Not her usual behavior. "Come on" I say, "Just a short ride up the keyhole and we'll return." Shane settles into herself, Charlie at her heels, to trot briskly up the single track. On our left the mountain rises, on our right a 50 foot drop to a dry creek bed. The dusty trail is but three foot wide. We are going too fast.

Before I can check her, my mare leaps. I hear rattling. I look back to see Charlie leap too. Over a huge snake, five to six feet in length, rattling its warning as it tries to cross the trail to the safety of the brushy cliff side. The dog looks back. I call for him.

The snake's rattling follows us as we descend to a wider part of the trail.

I feel exhilarated. I know all is well. That both animals are fine. I wrapped us all in white light before we left, but dutifully dismount to check them for puncture wounds. They are fine just excited. Not frothing with fear, but energized, ready to run. I know Snake has purposefully crossed my path.

On the way home I remember losing a day on the beaches of Mexico. I woke up feeling poisoned. My body ached, skin sensitive to the touch, nauseated, dizzy. Was it the sun? The margaritas? Dancing all night? I've done all before and never felt so sick, not hung over, but poisoned. Finally I purged the toxins onto the sand and slept the day away, dreaming serpentine images. Did I transmute snake medicine then?

Before I fall asleep that night, I set my intentions to dream of snake. *And Snake comes. This time lying flat on a platform, neatly folded in half, head to tail. I am observing in this dream. Participating yet also observing. I, as a young woman, kneel with a dustpan to sweep very close to the snake. I tell her to get back or the snake will strike. Without a warning rattle, Snake bites her right hand. I go to her and she transforms into a baby. I cradle her in my arms, the poison mottling*

7

her tender skin. Before I can take her to the emergency room, others try to kill the snake. They do a poor job and I stop them. I cannot save this snake, but I do kneel by its partially severed head and release its spirit with gratitude before finishing the kill. I take the head and slip it into a purse which rests against my solar plexus.

The doctors take their time in treating the baby. When they finally arrive it has been 22 hours since she was bitten. Her entire body is mottled yellowish green, yet she is conscious, cooing at me. A female physician takes a huge irrigation syringe filled with what looks like marinade and flushes the baby orally. The mottling disappears. I ask what is in the syringe. "Oh, it's lemon juice, orange juice, olive oil, hot pepper and melon!" Similar to my gallbladder flush recipe. The doctor smiles, "We do this for the parents. The child knows how to transmute the poison."

The baby has gotten up, transformed now to a toddler. She looks at me. It is me as a toddler…big green doe eyes, dark thick hair, and my child says to me the adult, "I have been transmuting poisons all my life."

I wake up in gratitude for Snake medicine.

4. SEVEN YEAR CYCLES

I am multi-sensory. We all are. Yet rarely admit it. Being clairsentient, clairvoyant, clairaudient is our nature, a soulful means of interpreting reality. When I was a little girl, I thought everyone felt the plants, heard the animals, saw the energies hovering over the earth and around people. I thought everyone had lucid dreams, knew the answers on tests, could tell what their parents were feeling in spite of their words. I still think we all have this capability. Yet most of us are taught that the world of the imaginal is just that…imagination. Not real.

I have a curious mind. My left brain is extremely active. I need to organize what I know. Bridge the gap between feeling and logic. I love numbers, math, patterns. There is a flow to life. Six months before my 50th birthday, I consulted with an astrologer who charted my life in 29 year lunar cycles. I was fascinated with the accuracy of interpretation. I was born under a tiny crescent moon on the Spring Equinox of 1961. My life has unfolded beautifully in seven year cycles…and it's happening again.

In 2003, I birthed my nutraceutical Genesis Gold® and my book LoveDance®. Both have changed my life dramatically. A week before Genesis Gold® was finally bottled my beloved old mare died, then a week after that, the man who helped me get my creation manufactured died. Death has preceded birth every single time…My life has unfolded in seven year cycles…like the phases of the moon…

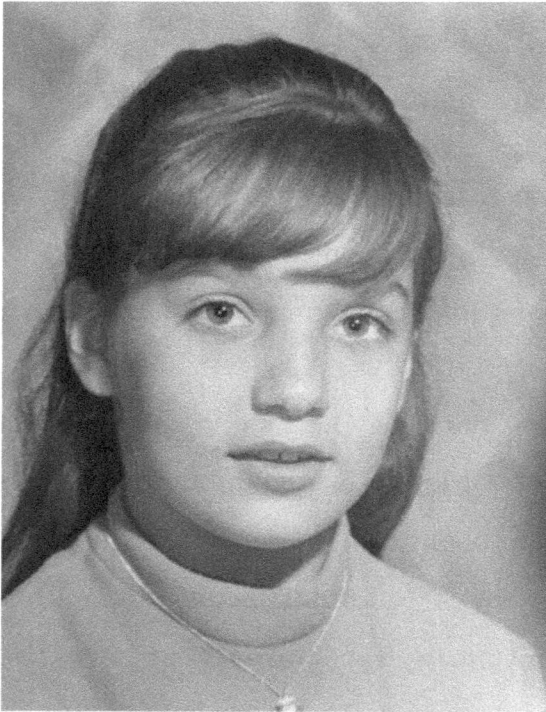

Third grade school picture 1969

September 26, 1969

I am eight years old. A great fire is raging in the dry hills behind our neighborhood. I am holding the ladder steady so my mother will not fall as she waters down our roof to prevent our house from catching fire. My sisters are watching television…the debut of The Brady Bunch…I really want to see it. Yet I am separated from the children. I am older than them…not just in age but my soul is older. All our neighbors are packing up their cars. They're leaving. My mother is very worried. My father is not here. In that moment as my mother's fear and anger pours down upon me like the smoke pouring down the hillside, I feel the weight of the world. The death of innocence…preceded the year before by the first death in my life. Our Easter bunny was killed by our Samoyed. Life is precious. You have to take care of the ones you love. I have spent the past seven years taking care of my parents and sisters. The next seven years, I learn how to depend solely on me.

Summer of 1975

I am fourteen. Walking with my sisters back to the pool. Poppop just bought us ice cream. Daddy is behind us talking to Pop. He calls up to me, "Debbie, your elbows are showing." I know exactly what he means. It is our family code for "your bathing suit has crept up your butt". Deftly I remedy the situation, yet this time I hear in his voice a different tone and I feel strange. Daddy sees me as a young woman. I look around me…three little sisters I am responsible for, a mother who feels diminished, a grandmother here on holiday but not here to support me through this time...she fears the blood as much as Momma, as much as every adult woman I know. I look at the ice cream dripping down my hand. This is the last ice cream I will ever eat. That moment I become anorexic. By the time I start high school, I'm twenty pounds lighter. My periods and breasts are gone. And I experience the second death...I find my mare's aborted foal and take it to school so my biology teacher can display it in a giant pickle jar. Science intrigues me. For seven years, I devote my energy to being the top in my class...fully cognizant that I am preparing for a career in health care...to legitimize my "knowing".

December, 1982

I am twenty-one. My beloved grandparents finally come to live in California. As soon as Poppop steps off the plane, I know he's dying. I cannot save him. Three weeks later we bury him. Only six months before I graduate from UCLA nursing school, I vow to never lose another patient. This begins a long cycle of my savior complex. It is seven years from Poppop's death before I see him in my dreams. Seven tough years of transition, loss, growth. Graduation, first job as an RN, getting married, moving away from home to begin a new life, birthing my son prematurely, getting my masters degree, birthing my daughter. Lots of birth followed Poppop's death. The cycle of birth and death well set now. My eating disorder has transformed from anorexia to bulimia. Only purging relieves me of the great pain of never being enough.

Spring of 1990

I am working as a family nurse practitioner at an urgent care. I pick up a chart and start to enter an exam room, but the doctor I'm working with takes the chart and hands me another. An HMO patient she doesn't want to see. Compensation is poor and her hands are tied within managed care. I don't want to be party to what I predict will become a managed care fiasco so I get involved with my professional nurse practitioner association and begin courting a private doctor. I spend six years under his employment making great money, increasing my skills and confidence while learning to balance motherhood, partnership, and career. Spiritually... a time of discovery... outside of the dogma I learned in the church. Still bulimia rules my days, sleep walking rules my nights, I can never do enough, be enough...

The death that preceded that birth cycle...our German Shepherd pup died suddenly in the fall of 1989. My husband was so broken hearted...Jarys consoled him on the back patio—put his little arm around his sobbing father's shoulders—told his father that souls are like rental videos that must be returned to

13

God....that night Poppop comes to me in a dream...the first time since he died.

September 5, 1996.

I am trying to resuscitate my daughter's puppy. Her screams fill my senses. Kyra dreamt its death. I console her with trepidation. My own dreams are so real, I act them out nearly every night. I am a sleepwalker. So thoroughly immersed in the obsessive compulsive nature of bulimia, I cannot do enough to keep from feeling so very deeply. I obsessively exercise as a competitive triathlete. My body fat is so low that I do not have periods. I am ready for change, tired of working as an employee in conventional medicine. So I create change...As a regional representative then state president of the California Coalition of Nurse Practitioners, I lead my colleagues to improve our professional status, like prescribing privileges and malpractice coverage for independent nurse practitioners. And in July of 1997, I birth my own private practice—Full Circle Family Health.

The cocoon for my greatest transformation, within Full Circle Family Health, I learn a great deal about holistic healing, the biochemistry of the neuro-immune-endocrine system, how to integrate alternative therapies with conventional medicine. I

14

develop a holistic model of Intuitive Integrative Medicine, collect loads of empirical data, create a nutritional product—Genesis Gold®—that would become the foundation of my healing practice. In fact Genesis Gold® would provide my hypothalamus with the necessary nutrients to finally heal my obsessive bulimic state of mind and more so, discover the psycho-spiritual roots of this dis-ease.

July 2002

We move to the house in my dreams…a little yellow house with white shutters…with room for my family, my horses and my practice. Finally I bring Full Circle Family Health home and begin living my most authentic life. Healing energy emanates from every corner of the property. Our animals serve therapeutic roles. Even the herb garden, the fruit trees and the flowers play their part in healing me, my family, my patients and my staff. Finally I am living my dreams.

And oh, yes…since I first consumed the Sacred Seven® amino acids…the formula that would become the secret sauce in Genesis Gold®… my sleep walking ceased. I slept peacefully through the night, began having regular periods, before starting the menopausal shift 5 years after my younger sisters. My bulimia abated as my obsessive compulsive nature mellowed.

More so, my soul growth has been profound…and unlike so many of the spiritual gurus I have treated over the years who suffered physically while seeking enlightenment, I have experienced optimal health physically, emotionally and mentally.

By the Spring Equinox 2011, I had completed seven – seven year cycles. Death filled the year before my 50th birthday—first Steve's Gran then two days later a beloved patient, and then Hope, our beloved Great Dane died on September 5th—fourteen years after Kyra's puppy. The last death was Bulimic Deb….

5. DANCING WITH MY SHADOW

On my son's 26th birthday, I released my shadow self. No longer do I feel the obsessive urges, the anxiety that can only be quelled through binging and purging. It's over. In the past I have been in recovery…during my two pregnancies and until my babies were weaned. Yet I struggled every day, became obsessive over every nutrient I consumed…not really free, only a temporary vacation from bulimia. And again, when I wrote LoveDance®.

For exactly eight months I obsessively wrote—420,000 words—yet as soon as the muse left me, bulimia found me.

At my women's retreat, I created a mask of my shadow self—Bulimic Deb—then danced with her before casting her into the flames...such a difficult thing to do. I mourned her death for weeks. I felt so profoundly afterwards. Every emotion I had not let myself feel—came in profound waves. Yet I was amazed at the underlying peace. I rode the waves of my emotions with a new found ease. I was at peace for the first time since I was 14.

After 35 years on and off the bulimic wagon, I was free.

What does that mean? To be free of bulimia. Well, I no longer obsess about food. I feel hunger and then I eat and for the first time enjoy each bite. I have my former trigger foods in my pantry. Not because I'm testing myself, but because I could not use all the chocolate chips I bought from Costco for my holiday baking. And I forget about them until the next time I feel like baking and am surprised to find a pound of chocolate chips...silent, no longer tempting me. Just me and chocolate happily co-existing. Not that I don't crave dark chocolate every moon cycle and I do indulge, gratefully consuming each luscious piece feeling my serotonin raising with each bite.

I've always associated eating disorders with addictions. Such a horrible addiction because you cannot abstain from food, like you can from alcohol or drugs. And when I was bulimic, I had to abstain especially from my trigger foods. Over the past few years I desensitized myself by ritualizing my trigger foods. I started with dark chocolate. I ate it ceremoniously on fine china with a glass of red wine on a table set with lace under candle light while watching a feel good movie. All my senses were engaged in pleasure and from then on (that was in 2008) I have been able to consume dark chocolate in moderation without it triggering a binge. Not so milk chocolate...so that's why forgetting about having chocolate chips in the house amazes me.

I do have one regret. When I cast my mask into the flames (and I was the last to do it...reluctant to let Bulimic Deb go) I felt the smoke was carried elsewhere. So two months later at Thanksgiving, I was not surprised to see one of my nieces bone thin and stuffing her face...the family curse, my sister calls it. An unresolved karmic imprint, I believe.

I do not feel guilt or shame related to food or my body. In fact, I love my body. I am so grateful for this beautiful healthy body that has taught me my greatest lessons, protected me from my greatest fears, blessed me by being the most perfect vehicle for my transformation. After seven years in a cocoon of my making, I am emerging as a butterfly.

And I no longer feel like purging my emotions. Now I feel them, really sit within my heart to be with my emotions. And I have found a profound gratitude for my rich passionate emotions. So powerful they seem to control the weather. Or at least the climate of my relationships. And with this awareness, I have learned to ride the wave of my emotions…and let them go into the ocean of feeling that makes me human and connects me to all that is.

6. NAKED BARBIE ON A BRYER HORSE

When I was a little girl my sisters and I played Barbies. Each birthday or Christmas, we would ask for a Barbie implement to share — the Malibu beach condo, the cool Barbie camper, a huge Barbie house complete with skididdle kiddles for babies and my absolute favorite — Bryer Horses! Well, the youngest took over the condo and the Malibu Ken, one twin claimed the camper while the other got the big house and the babies. I got the Horse. Since shoes didn't stay on Barbie while astride her Arabian stallion and the youngest sister was a clothes hog, well, I played Naked Barbie on a Bryer Horse.

Are we always the same from childhood to adulthood? The patterns run strong in my family. The youngest married "Malibu Ken" and lives that life. The camper twin has traveled the world and never really settled down. The other twin lives in a big house with four daughters. I still ride the horse ☺

And I live naked…baring my soul as part of my healing work.
I had a vision. During a guided meditation in my women's circle, I saw myself being born from the heart of the earth. A golden woman on a blood red horse with amethyst wings furled on her back. The embodiment of my Higher Self.
Now, I am no longer Naked Barbie on Bryer Horse. I have wings! Like a butterfly emerging from a cocoon after a lifetime of binging like a caterpillar, I am transformed.

7.   BY ANY OTHER NAME…

I was born Deborah Lee Perry. An unusual name for an Italian-American girl. Most of the first born girls in my mother's family were name Marie, but my mother, Maria, insisted that I be named Deborah. She remembered getting a lot of flack for wanting to christen her daughter with a Jewish name. My father remembers that it was the closest female name to his given name. Although my mother always called me Deborah, I quickly got nicknamed, Debbie.

So I entered Honby elementary school as Debbie Perry. That's when I met my first friend.

We met in second grade. She was the youngest of four girls; I was the oldest. Her sisters were all grown up; mine were just starting school. We lived in two different neighborhoods separated by a four lane highway. We had little in common, but seven year olds don't care. We both loved our teacher, Mrs Groves, who smelled like oranges and liked to take naps under the art table while we were at recess. We both loved books. What a great day it was when she got her first pair of glasses and we got to be in the same reading group.

After reconnecting, we reminisced over lunch. She laughed remembering me wagging my finger at the class bully at recess. I had researched the word that he used so cruelly and taught him and the rest of the kids who gathered around us the true meaning of the F-word. I got called into the principal's office. Since I had never been in trouble before I was scared but argued my point until Mom arrived. The principle asked what she had been teaching me. The truth, Mom said. Even the principle was not aware of the naval origin of the word.

With her sisters out of the house, my friend was treated like an only child. I, on the other hand, had to share everything with my three little sisters. She had cool lunches — a Wonder bread sandwich, a miniature bag of Fritos and a shiny silver wrapped DingDong. While I had leftovers on wheat bread, chips in a baggy and a piece of fruit. She had her own bedroom with pretty curtains that matched her bedspread and lots of toys. I shared a bunk bed with my little sister, the twins in matching bunks in the same room until my aunt and my two cousins moved out.

Although we had precious little time to catch up, I bared my soul to my oldest friend.

Starting kindergarten worried me. Who would watch after my sisters while I was gone? The white light! I remembered that I called the white light around me whenever I felt lost, worried or frightened and was instantly protected. Sometimes the white light was so bright that I felt invisible, no one seemed to notice me. I would surround my sisters with the white light of protection. They would be perfectly safe until I returned from school.

She remarked that I always seemed more mature than the rest of our class. Perhaps that was being the eldest child. Perhaps it's just being an old soul.

From the moment we reconnected, she called me Deborah...not Debbie as everyone else from my past still does. I asked her why. She said that I am no longer little Debbie...She perceived my transformation. Perhaps someday, my family of origin will too.

She wrote afterwards: "I didn't realize how much I was missing you in my life. We've both grown tremendously in our years apart and have so much to share. I think about some of the things you shared with me, and it makes me sad that I didn't know your burdens and wasn't more supportive. How well did we really know each other? All I knew was you were my friend and I loved you

And I responded: "Please do not worry about the past. I did not even remember much of my childhood drama until after I gave birth. I do remember how much I loved you! It did not matter that we didn't know each other intimately, we knew each other's souls...and that was enough to become best friends. Love you still!"

Friends are gifts. Love them as much as you can.

Dancing with Kyra, 1989

8. SPIRIT ON A HUMAN JOURNEY

This life is not a spiritual journey. This is a human journey. My spirit chose this form to know itself as divine. But in answer to my friend's question, it seems I began calling it a spiritual journey in 1997 when I opened my private health care practice. Full Circle Family Health. The physical manifestation of a dream.

I have dreamt every significant thing in my life. My beloved husband. My enlightened children. All my creations. Then perceiving the music, the vibration, the energy, I dance my dreams into reality. And as a holistic family nurse practitioner, I dance healing with my patients.

After nine years of gathering health care experience as an employee, I prayed to be shown a way to fulfill my soul purpose. I had a dream...to start my own holistic health care practice. I dreamt of my patients walking down a garden path into a healing home, where I had the space to practice truly integrated medicine and enough time to spend with my precious family, animals, and garden — dancing my dream.

Soon after Full Circle Family Health became a reality, the universe sent me the most challenging patients. Out of necessity and a great desire to know more, I became an expert in neuro-immune-endocrinology, a specialty which focuses on the bio-chemical communication network of the human body. It's always about proper communication, isn't it?

Well, I opened myself to receive whatever the universe might offer. The sickest most Hormonally Challenged patients came from all over California for my care. As my expertise grew, patients came from across the United States and then from Europe and South America. Word of mouth referrals kept me very busy.

Then I began getting referrals from energy healers. One in particular referred her clients for hormonal support. I was happy to comply. And very curious. This energy healer sent her clients to me with such precise descriptions of what was energetically going on in their bodies that I was able to scientifically assess and diagnose their dis-eases. Her clients got better — physically and energetically — and soon she became my patient.

Annette was very open to everything I could teach her about her body. She was going through menopause and needed hormonal support. I wanted to learn about her work. So we bartered.

My first session with Annette found me sitting across from her in a lotus position, eyes closed, hands resting in the "ok" position on my knees. She began to laugh. "You don't remember who you are."

"What do you mean? Am I not doing it right?"

"This is not your way. Go run with that black dog of yours." How did she know about Ida? "And when she stops, follow her lead and sit down with her. See what comes."

So I did. I was an avid runner and enjoyed racing across the trails with my dog. I rarely stopped to smell the roses let alone sit down. But I followed Annette's advice. When Ida jumped up onto a huge boulder and sat down to look at me, I climbed up to sit by her, closed my eyes, took a deep breath and…a purple tear dropped into my mind's eye, filled my head, spilled into every aspect of my being…and the answer to a problem came very clearly to me. Wow!

Soon I was meditating in my way. While I ran with my dog, rode my horse, danced in the garden...always the purple tear drop came and with it answers. I began to remember who I am.

9. SPIRITUAL GURUS

After meeting Annette, I started to barter services with other spiritual gurus. To me they were gurus. They had a name for their gifts, unabashedly used the energy and charged a great deal for their services. It's true that I used my intuition to diagnose and treat my patients. They trusted me or rather my intuition. And I had diagnostic tests to "prove my knowing". Annette said I was still in the closet.

"How do you think you diagnose them so easily?"

When I started my private practice, I wasn't ready to admit that I used the energies to diagnose my patients. But it was true that none of my colleagues seemed to be able to "hear" the carotid bruits that only Dopplers detected. Nor could they "smell" the cancer in our patients later confirmed by pathology. Even the gynecologist I worked with could not "feel" the cysts that he could only find with a laparoscope. One physician would perform surgery based on my "findings". He did not wish for the others to know, but when I described tumors to a tenth of a centimeter that he found in the operating room, he too was a believer. Yet I had not come out to them.

So I saw one of Annette's colleagues. She too was hormonally challenged, one of the most physically frail people I had ever met. More ether than substance. I was curious as to her "abilities", yet certainly did not wish to trade my strength and vitality for her ethereal experiences. It's as if she could not physically hold all the energy she was bringing in to this dimension. She's not the only one, just my first encounter.

So after I got her hormonally balanced, I went to her for a session. I did not know what to expect. Annette's sessions reminded me of Healing Touch—an energy therapy started by holistic nurses to certify health care professionals. Anika's sessions were more like channeling. And she said, that never before had so much information came in. She was not the only energy healer/channel that related amazing transmissions during our time together. I thought it was them. My mother said it was me.

As soon as I sat in front of Anika, I felt a winged presence behind me. Anika described it as a seraph. I felt embraced, held, protected. I "heard" the being's name—Constantina—and it "said" she had been with me since the beginning. Although Anika related some of this through her channeling, my own imagery and sensory experience filled in the gaps, making this very real for me. "Constantina" assured me that I was not to worry about Steve. I was to step forth on the path before me and trust that he would follow.

What a great relief to have my greatest fear addressed. I was afraid that if I forged ahead on my spiritual journey that I would leave my beloved behind. My fear was mirrored in my husband's distrust of Anika and the other spiritual gurus to follow. He tolerated Annette but she respected him. The others did not. Some even advised that if I was to achieve enlightenment in this lifetime that I had to leave him. I left them instead.

One thing I know is Love. My husband loves me with all his heart and I love him. If this was the right path, then we would take it together. Well, more like in tandem. Rather me going first and him following. He told me once that he was a gatekeeper. He felt his job was to be sure that everyone he loved got through.

He knew I was a leader. He encouraged me to grow, to explore, to learn, to make change. He said if I kept looking back for him, we would never get anywhere.

Now at the time, I felt held back by my love. But the more I got to know the gurus, the more I realized that their "gifts" were not worth all they gave up. Most of these women lived alone. They did not have significant others in their lives—no husbands, no lovers, no close friends, no children. They had left everything they knew to follow their path.

I felt so strongly that everything I knew and loved were part of me. I was willing to go first, to lead the way, but I vowed not to leave them behind. Constantina's message was very reassuring. Since then I have come to see that leading is flying in triangular formation like a flock of geese. One goose is up front with a clear view of where the flock is going. All the rest of the geese are just flying nose to tail, trusting that the leaders know the way. I am not alone. The other outer geese are there. Sometimes that goose is my husband. Flying up from the rear to relieve me.

Steve and me on our 31st anniversary

10. SOULMATES

When I was sixteen, I wrote a letter to God. In the midst of my anorexia, feeling abandoned by spirit, I told God in no uncertain terms that in spite of my mission on earth if my beloved did not show up soon, I would not make it.

Soon after I met my soul mate in a dream...long golden curls, sky blue eyes, the body of Adonis...I awoke with hope and wonder. Where was he?

Suddenly my parents decided that my high school was too far away (I rode the bus over an hour and half to get there every day) and the growing tension between the white and black kids was not the best environment for my younger sisters (although I had been going to this interracial school for two and half years and learned to make friends with the leaders of the black girls who looked out for me). So in the spring of my junior year I left all my friends and transferred to the high school closest to my parents' business.

And on the first morning of track practice, we were told to partner with another athlete to stretch. All the other kids quickly found a partner. I turned to my left and there He was. Sky blue eyes, long golden curls, body of Adonis with a very Greek name to match—Stefanos Darius Maragopoulos—but everyone called him Steve.

The first time I looked into his eyes, I knew.

My soul mate. The one I dreamt. The one I asked God to send.

We were only kids! What was God thinking?

It took awhile to settle into the gift. We don't always receive gifts right away. We question our worth. We wonder how it's possibly going to work out. We thank the Divine and question It at the same time. At least I did.

Steve and I took our time getting reacquainted with one another. He was very patient for a sixteen-year-old. We talked about everything. We are both first born. He had two brothers. I had three sisters. His family was very poor. Mine was middle class. He was being raised by a single mother...divorced twice from abusive relationships. His father was somewhere in Greece. Although it seemed that I had raised myself, my parents were still together. My family loved him.

The summer before my senior year in high school, my grandparents came from Philadelphia. The first time they met Steve, Poppop kissed him. My grandparents were very Italian and men kissed each other. All my sisters' boyfriends were put off by this custom. Not Steve.

A good Greek boy, Steve welcomed Pop's kiss. Una raza, una faza. One race, one face. When Steve returned the embrace, Pop took me aside and said, "You better keep this one, Poppy." I did.

Recently our firstborn asked how to know if the person you're attracted to is The One. I told him it came down to the first feeling you have when you meet. Jarys asked what I felt when I met his Dad. I remember so clearly. I felt Safe.

Safe to unveil my heart and be my truth. Since that fateful ice cream cone. I had used my anorexia to hide Me. There was no hiding with Steve. I revealed everything. Even the ugly parts. And he accepted all of me. He loved me unconditionally. I had never known love like his.

Steve said that the feeling he had when he first met me was…Home. He felt that he had come home. He still feels the same and so do I.

And when I look into his sky-blue eyes, I see myself as Love.

All we have been through over the past 38 years…the deaths, the divorces, the difficult decisions, the challenging careers, the tremendous soul growth that often feels like we have lived many lives in one...all has been transformed into joy. I counsel a lot of people and as a police officer and a coach, so does Steve.

We are eternally grateful for being together this long and still so very much in love. We are best friends, still passionately attracted to each other, great partners in creating our amazing life. I used to see myself as ahead of him on our spiritual path...yet no more, for clearly we are in tandem...taking turns leading when the other needs a rest. And family, friends, and strangers come to us for advice on relationships. And all I can say is how we got here is by choosing Love.

Part Two
DANCING DREAMS

11. MAY I HAVE THIS DANCE?

Sultry music warms the desert air. And I've been dancing—Brazilian Samba—all night. Once, twice with my beloved, but dancing is not his thing. It's mine. I cannot keep still when the drum calls. I dance with whoever asks. Men, women, children...or just with the drummer.

All my sisters and my mother came with me to this Cinco de Mayo celebration in the rosy desert glow of Palm Springs. Our dear friends invited us to partake of their Mexican feast, margaritas and music. Most of the celebrants are gay...and I am in heaven with no shortage of dance partners. Although my mother ventured onto the dance floor, my sisters kept to themselves, later wondering why they danced so little. At the intermission, the band leader told me why.

He had put on some recorded music and the other dancers left. Still captivated by the energy, I stayed. He asked me to dance.

When I slipped into his arms, he made a comment, "Your body is perfect for dancing."

And I said, "My husband is right over there."

He laughed. "Forgive me. I have been watching you dance all night. Partnering with dancers of all abilities. And each one you received and danced with beautifully. Your body is perfect for dancing."

Perhaps he's right. I have yet to encounter a person I cannot dance with. I just follow their lead. They may be awkward or shy or overly trained in a particular style of dance that may not match the music. It doesn't matter. Somehow their inner dancer comes out to dance with me.

Years ago, I attended a Science and Consciousness conference in New Mexico. The conference began with Dances of Universal Peace. A large group of us circled around a makeshift band of musicians with drums, flutes and stringed instruments. I was enchanted. The music was so enticing. I danced joyously with each and every one in the circle. And many people approached me afterwards complimenting me on my dancing. "Are you a professional dancer?" I just laughed. Far from it.

I never thought of myself as a dancer. In fact, my husband used to tease that I danced to the beat of a different drummer. But I didn't care, enjoying the music, the camaraderie, the energy. I called my guru friend. I thought Anika would love the dances, especially since she had been taking ballroom dancing and had started dancing competitively. She huffed at the idea that anyone would think I was a professional dancer. "You've had no training!"

Hmm. I didn't know what to say. But since then I have had many people express enchantment at my dancing. Then I wrote LoveDance® and finally understood.

Dancing is my way of connecting with the energy. A means of celebration, of expressing my feelings, of being present. And life is a dance of love. Steve suggested that LoveDance® is my expression of Self. Love is at the center of the triad of Relationships, Soul Purpose, and Health. I include Health because as a Holistic Nurse Practitioner, Health of Body, Mind, and Soul is paramount in the Process of Enlightenment. It is not enough for me to talk...but to walk my talk...or rather...to dance my truth!

12. PARTNERING WITH MY PATIENTS

After nine years of working as an employee first at an urgent care then with an ob-gyn, I had a dream...to start my own holistic health care practice.

So I left a private practice seeing 27 or more patients a day as an employee to slow down and spend quality time with my own patients; time that they gratefully compensated me for and then submitted their completed bill of services to their own insurance. Finally I was independent of the insurance industry. Soon a trend began as patients invested in their care became increasingly more responsible for their health.

My dearest patients supported my entrepreneurial nature by following me into my new integrative medical practice—Full Circle Family Health. One day I was evaluating a woman with postmenopausal bleeding and had an uneasy feeling. A few years earlier my intuition led me to discover a rare growth on her liver. She trusted my feelings and did not hesitate to agree to an ultrasound. That's when we discovered the tumor.

I had diagnosed patients with cancer before. I had even lost a few to the disease. But this beloved patient was different. Her cancer became our dance floor. I learned to partner with Barbara to the rhythm of her dis-ease, to the changing beat of her desire, to the symphony of her life's purpose.

I held nothing back, dancing with her through choices that I may not have chosen, orchestrating a care plan that fit her needs — physically, emotionally, mentally and spiritually. I researched every option, conventional and alternative. She fought the good fight, but in the end…she showed me how to slow dance.

On the morning of her death, I felt Barbara as a bubble of delight floating through me. Not an hour later, her daughter called to tell me she had just passed. For the first time in 25 years of healing, I experienced the grace of death.

Like most health care professionals, I had viewed death of a patient as a failure and could not fully receive the gift of their passing. But hers, I embraced. I surrendered to loving her as a person, to getting close to her family, to being a part of her circle — truly Full Circle Family Health.

At the funeral, others commended me for coming. How could I not? I came to honor her, to support her family and to let her go. Like many of her loved ones, I shared my thoughts. Mostly I thanked her delightful spirit, free now from pain playing with her little grandson.

This is the way it used to be. Before insurance carriers and malpractice, we used to get involved with our patients. We knew their families, we birthed them, we helped them get through tough times in their lives, and we buried them. We understood the circle of life. They understood too. We respected one another; we were part of a community.

As I dance my dreams into reality, they expand to encompass all I love. Transforming my health care practice into one that supports my relationships, my health and my soul purpose— my LoveDance® — has allowed me to model a healthy balanced life which helps my patients achieve their goals. And those who are ripe for healing arrive from across the globe.

They come because I dance their dance.

13. THE RED CORD

Writing my novel helped me heal the Mother Wound...the original separation from the Divine Mother...as my heroine Mary Magdalen awakened to her truth as the Divine Daughter...so did I...and in doing so received the fullness of the Divine Mother.

I reconnected to Her...embodied in the Earth...enlivened in the hearts of so many women here in Ojai...mothers and grandmothers who receive me...as if I am the Divine Daughter...and I feel it. I see the Divine Daughter energy in so many others...women young and old and even a few precious men.

Nearly three years after LoveDance® was launched, I found myself facing another wound...the Father Wound — separation from the Divine Father. Yes, I had begun Book II... LoveDance® is a trilogy...and I began the second book shortly after the first was launched...I got 1/3 through the writing...and just as my heroine Mary Magdalen confronts her father wound...I could write no more!

Why? Because until I face it, live it, breathe it, am I able to write it. What I wrote in the first book became manifest for me. I did not realize the depth of the mother wound I embodied, imprinted since prenatal time, brought into this lifetime as deep karmic imprints. I had done a regression on myself many years before. Way before LoveDance® …two years before I dreamt I was Mary Magdalen walking down the streets of Nazareth, I brought myself back to the womb...Disentangled myself from maternal karmic imprints… from the Red Cord…

Looking down between my fetal thighs, I was surprised to see NO penis! No blade! How could I accomplish my mission in this form? I felt a pulsation deep in my belly, putrid fearful, coming not from me, but through the umbilical cord – the Red Cord.

It was my mother's fear. I felt her. Her world as she perceived it...the struggle with her parents, her new husband, her fear…her fear of her mother, then…

I was in my grandmother's womb feeling her fear through the red cord. And then in her mother's womb feeling her mother's fear and her mother's and back and back in time. Like a video montage, yet I could feel the fear…yellow and acidic as bile…the pain, tears, terror…of losing children, abortions, stillborn babies.

Of being raped, used as chattel, traded like beasts. Of husbands, and fathers and lovers beating us, blaming us. Of too many babies, of hunger and pain, of sending our sons off to war and our daughters into the same traps we found ourselves. Of burning at the stake, of drowning, of torture for being our truth. Of giving away our power.

Through my mother's womb, through hers, and unto the beginning of time. Back to Eve. All of women's woes…that was my fear. The fear I had been purging forever.

Time to release it.

I awoke with a clear intention and pure desire to release my mothers' fear, all of my mothers.

In synchronicity that same day, I had an appointment with an energy healer. She was working with another powerful male healer. He stood at my feet, she at my head. I didn't tell them of my vision, but lay there fully intending to release. And I did. Like a volcanic eruption of black tar, the energy exploded from my belly into the atmosphere. I felt lighter and freer than ever. I opened my eyes laughing and sat up.

The two healers were plastered against the walls of the healing room. "What was THAT?"

"That was fear! And it's not mine!"

Then I headed to the beach, and lay on the sand, my feet in the water, the sun on my naked skin and was held by the Great Mother. My Divine Mother loves me...I am everything she ever desired in a daughter.

I no longer need to purge the fear of my sex.

14. FOUR FACES OF THE ONE

As I waited for Genesis Gold® to be manufactured I sat down to write my opus — Hormones in Harmony® — what I was known for, all my healing secrets. Yet it wasn't coming easily. In spite of all the case studies and stories, I could not seem to get it down. And I am a prolific writer. I have a whole cedar chest filled with my handwritten journals, poetry, short stories, novelettes...yet what I do best was not coming...

February 1st, 2003

Finally I sat in meditation, awakening early by the light of the day while my animal charges continued to slumber. Upon my couch I sat still and quiet and within moments and lasting what seemed an eternity I was visited. The Father, the Mother, the Son and the Daughter came unto me. I envisioned their form through closed eyes, yet felt them intimately interacting with my physical being, touching my aura within and without.

The Father held the space balancing the energy confirming the wisdom of the Mother and Son. The Daughter was beautiful to behold and when I asked who she was I was told Shekhina and I saw that she was a huge version of Me! Full voluptuous body, moving gracefully through space and time, glowing with a golden love light dancing sensuously to the vibration of the moment. She had my face, my hair, my eyes, she was me lovely to behold.

The Mother gave me her wisdom through counsel and vibration. When I asked what I was to do, she said I had done enough that all was progressing as it should, that Genesis Gold® would come in its own time as divinely planned. I was to write, only write. I asked which books to begin with and she said there is one book, all the stories are part of the one. My story, all of it.

Not <u>Hormones in Harmony®</u> separately, but inclusive as is my understanding. The Son concurred stating that unlike Christ my true story would come out while I was still alive and the work would unfold from the telling of it.

I was told that I was to use my gift in energy healing to minister to a patient- Eddie- whose cancer was based in his fear, that I would be guided as to what physical support systems he would need and that yes, Genesis Gold® was necessary, but would come too late. I know that people come into my life for a purpose, some to stay and some for just fractions of eternity. All part of the web of love connected with the white gold filaments of alchemized truth.

The Mother guided me to understand that like a teenage girl, I needed many mirrors to assure myself of my truth and confirm what I perceived as blemishes, as imperfections. Those I call my mentors have been these mirrors for me. They guide me with such finesse, because I am witnessing myself.

It is my connectedness that makes their counsel, their channeling, their energy healing so profound. It is me.

15. DEATH AND THE WHITE LIGHT

Eddie. He came to me in the fall of 2002, diagnosed with lung cancer. His lawyer, a patient of mine, suggested he consult with me. I was the clinical endocrine advisor in a research project using natural progesterone to treat cancer at the Sansum Medical Clinic so she thought I could help him.

Cancer is not my specialty. I specialize in neuro-immune-endocrinology which I believe is at the core of most dis-ease. So I spent two hours going over his history, looking for signs of age-related decline that could be at the root of his illness, trying to understand why this brilliant man's body was failing him at 52, and explaining the biochemistry of cancer as related to the complicated system of hormonal miscommunication with DNA.

Exuding enthusiasm, Eddie asked, "So you have something to balance my ligands?" He was brilliant, one of the only patients who understood the scientific lingo of my theories. He was even open to the psycho-spiritual roots of dis-ease, including the irony of being afflicted with cancer after inventing thermal implants to treat brain tumors.

In fact, I did have something—a formula to balance the hypothalamic orchestration of the neuro-immune-endocrine system—but, in theory only. After completing pilot studies the year before, my personal funds ran out and I struggled to find a manufacturer to mix even a small batch. Eddie took my hand and offered to help.

"No," I protested, "you came here for me to help you."

"Perhaps I came to help you. My cancer was a fortuitous portal for our meeting."

Thus began our journey to manufacture my formula so he might partake of it. He truly believed he would be cured by my invention. In the meantime, I researched natural treatment regimens, since he was opposed to conventional therapies, and spent much time counseling him and sharing many spiritual portals. He treated me as a beloved daughter, introducing me to colleagues who would forge the path to the birth of my nutraceutical product. Becoming attached, I searched for cures for his cancer.

The day I brought the first bottle of Genesis Gold® to him, he smiled, beckoned me closer and whispered, "I knew you could do it."

It was his last lucid moment. At the request of his family I had been coming to his lovely villa in the hills of Santa Barbara to help him die. As a nurse practitioner, I treated the walking well. Some patients had passed over the years, usually of old age, occasionally untimely, but not since being a neophyte nurse had I witnessed death.

After graduating nursing school in 1983, I worked on a surgical floor at UCLA Medical Center. We saw the sickest of patients — heart transplants, complete surgical resections of the bowels, lung resections. My first encounter with death was a young woman, my age, dying of pancreatic cancer. When I arrived on the night shift and saw her Do Not Resuscitate order, I knew her family and physicians had given up.

Not me! I was not going to let her drown in her own secretions and stayed by her bedside suctioning her tracheostomy. Her intern refused to give me a permanent suction order so that I would take care of my other three patients, so I handed him the suction catheter and called the chief resident. My colleagues were appalled. No one called the chief in the middle of the night, especially not a nurse.

Amazingly, he wasn't upset, but asked if I saw the DNR order. "Doctor, I'm not resuscitating her. I just don't want her to be alone. I..." Seeing the intern escape down the hall, I tried to hang up on the chief.

"Oh, no, you don't. We're going to discuss why you can't let her die." I resisted, but he kept me on the phone until it was too late.

The charge nurse helped me prepare the young woman's body for the morgue. And with tears, I was forced to let my patient go.

Twenty years later, I was not so resistant. Eddie's family left me alone with him. I sat at his bedside and meditated on how I could help him pass. I had already counseled with each of his family members. When I thought of his recalcitrant son who had finally agreed to see his father after our phone conversation that morning, I felt a wave of gratitude. And it wasn't mine, it was from Eddie. I opened my eyes.

His diminished energy, faded to non-existent in his limbs, now concentrated in his heart chakra, shimmered, and I gasped to see a funnel of light connect to him. He appeared to lift from his form — pure white light not the fiery red of his life force — and enter the conical shaped energy. Other light forms greeted him, ancestors and guides, passing him along to the end. And at the infinite end of this brilliant white light was pure Love. He was enveloped, embraced like long lost lovers, the encounter so intimate; I was torn between turning away in deference to such a private moment and watching in awe.

Suddenly, Eddie's essence turned away from the Light and I was swept up into his perspective. It appeared as if the room where his body lay with me at his bedside, existed in a fishbowl. The reality was the Light, the physical existence, an illusion. So peaceful, so blissful, the Light was very familiar to me.

I remembered calling in the White Light to protect my little sisters while I was away at kindergarten and invoking the same White Light to surround my own children whenever I dropped them off for school. If I would forget, my daughter would remind me, "Mommy, do the White Light," and I would swaddle her and her brother in the protection of the Light that had always comforted me. In that eternal moment, I recalled how the same White Light seemed to bathe my patients and me during a healing and was the one I used to calm injured animals before I treated them.

I had never been afraid of dying, although letting others go was difficult. My fear lay in being alone, separated from those I love by death. As a healer, I had taken a very long time to release my savior complex, to understand that I was not responsible for my patients' illnesses, nor could I take credit for their cures. I was a midwife to their healing, holding the space in which they recovered or not—it was their choice.

That night after his son came to his bedside to say goodbye, Eddie died.

Two months later, I received my greatest opening and began writing my life's work. Never a moment of writer's block, it all just flowed in. The synchronicity of events, from the creative process, to publishing, to going out in the world to market has been amazing. Still, I am learning to ask for help and whenever I feel resistant, I hear Eddie, "Perhaps I am here to help you," and open to receive another's assistance.

Witnessing the rehearsal of his death was Eddie's final gift to me. Death is a passing through the veil of illusion and into the truth. There is nothing to fear.

16. SEEDS OF INTENTION

At the fall meeting of the Ojai Grandmother's Council, we were reminded of the seeds of intention that we planted in the spring. Some could not remember their intentions, some remembered but did not tend them. I was acutely aware of mine. My birthday is on the Spring Equinox and every year I plant seeds of intention with the hopes of a great harvest come fall. That year my intention was to be open to receive abundance.

Oh, I have much. My life is very rich. A beautiful home, fertile land, healthy, happy children, an amazing relationship with my beloved husband, a fulfilling healthcare practice, yet I feel that there is more…that I am to go out into the world and share my wisdom…and to do that…I need resources…money and people to help…and although my business pays the bills, there is debt incurred to build the practice, to manufacture Genesis Gold®…and my book — LoveDance® — waiting for release.

Since planting my seeds of intention, I'd been acutely aware of the abundance in my life, living in gratitude as the universe has seen fit to challenge me…with death, and loss, and sacrifice. As if I had to empty my Soul Purse over and over to make room for the abundance to come.

That night… I have sequence of five dreams…

All the time I'm dreaming, I'm lucid. I fall in and out of sleep after a tremendous hot flash at 12:30 — three hours after I fell asleep — and spend time rolling around considering what I should do about my hormonal challenge…then set my intention to know what it's all about at the soul level and fall asleep…

…The first dream opens with a gathering of women in a great big house. I'm trying to settle in and my roommate shows up. One of my young patients and she's distraught, hands me her pants. She needs another pair just like them. I tell her pants are expensive in…Italy…wow, that's where we are!... and she hands me $50. I look at the pants…olive green suede polyester nothing wrong with them except a blood stain at the crotch. She is mortified that she started her period…this is the patient I saw last week who missed her period…I explain she can wash them out, but she will never wear them again — stained with women's blood…I am saddened by her shame, I want to make it better for her…and then I see that she is me as a girl not at peace with my femininity and all women afraid they are unclean as the

world has treated them. And I feel a deep sense of gratitude for finally embracing my feminine power...

...and the dream shifts. I'm with the same gathering, but so crowded, too many women... A fake sense of feminine power emanates from them – over inflated, dangerous – a roomful of women wearing pants under skirts. I need to get away. But it's so crowded. Finally, I remember I can fly! I start to push off away from the crowded staircase...and another woman, one from my women's circle...says "Hold her!" I am chased by two women, struggling to gain altitude through the crowded place, they grasp my trailing legs, but cannot catch me. I feel light but too low...the energy is one of a dog teasing its owners into a game of chase-- I head for the light, but they close the opening before I can fly there...I'm trapped in a great big tent! ...Lucid, I try to wake up...and realize until I get the message of the dream sequence, I'm not going anywhere...I fly up through ropes, tight ropes. Below me, all the women I've gotten involved with in this life and beyond – from girls scouts, to sorority sisters, to the nurse practitioners I led, and the women's circle, the grandmothers, and interspersed are the women gurus who wove in and out of my life these past 13 years...all who wanted me to join them, to lead them... ...my lucid self so happy to be flying again (I haven't flown in my dreams since the women's retreat just before the Autumn Equinox where we worked on our karmic imprints)...How funny that my subconscious traps me in a circus tent with crazy women. I laugh...

....and slip into another dream. A great gathering of all my dead patients. Everyone's there...Eddie in the background – smoking! – Lacy, Michael, many whose names I've forgotten but not their faces – whole and healthy – and their energy. All doing whatever they please...peace emanates from them. The last patient I buried is there too. A sense of guilt carried from my waking world trickles into my dreamtime. Barbara is the spokeswoman and she's explaining where Anna is on her spirit path so soon after her death. "There is no need for regret. You danced your best dance with each of us. We are where we need to be at this time in human consciousness." Gran's there too. And she is walking very strangely...like she's in a space suit, sort of praying mantis like. I wonder if her walker would help, and Gran apologizes...it's broken, how difficult it is to move on earth, so much easier over there. I have a catalog in my hands and pick out a handicap toilet for her...pink and orange!...which seems silly since I know Gran isn't staying...and feel bad that we didn't make these accommodations for her while she was alive. I show her the toilet. "I never had such a bright toilet!" she says, "but I don't think I'll need one. I'm not staying, dear. This is the first time you let me in." True, she has visited Steve many times. I inquire about the others. She says "I have very nice visits with Steve, but the rest are harder." I hope she isn't spending too much time and effort trying to contact those who are not ready to receive her. She laughs and says, no she is very busy over there, but not to worry. Time is not an issue for her anymore and effort, well it is easier to be in

the presence of love than fear… In my observer, lucid dreamer state, I
want to spend more time with the dead, knowing it's precious…it's the
first time I've dreamt of Gran and she feels so real…our conversations
though bizarre yet so genuine. The only one I miss in the dreams is
Hope…she's not with the grateful dead…but I'm not sad. I know my
beloved Great Dane, my Hope, is where she belongs…

…then I'm on a huge field, tossing a yellow grass-stained nerf football
to a black dog and a blond boy. Every pass, they switch off, I'm not a
good thrower and neither of them catch well. We pass through many
other people's games/lives, communicate with them and move on. All
are men and boys…fathers and sons. Playing amongst a group of black
men and boys, one of which compliments my butt as I bend over the
tub to find the dog tied up like a broken doll almost fetal like. I keep
finding its limp body left behind with the ball underwater. At first I
dismiss the comment as I did in my youth with an excuse and then I
replay the scene and graciously thank the man and he swells and
merges with the other black men, their sons receiving their vibration as
the sacred feminine received them…back to the fetal dog and used up
ball left underwater…I realize the boy has moved on… this boy-dog
issue I know is mine…my inner boy child leaving me and the spirit dog
connecting him to the otherworld left behind…this is part of the healing
the divine masculine within me…

…then I'm back in the house — my recurring house dream. Usually in the "house" dream, I am so frustrated…my sisters keep me from getting what I need to get done, I'm always cooking or cleaning and everything is a disaster…this time I am just watching while being in the midst of them…like I'm watching a home movie while being in it … this time, instead of wandering the never-ending rooms, and halls, I stay in the kitchen-family room where all the family is gathered. It's our rental, yet I have no sense of ownership… The family has rented it before and now have a disaster with the microwave. I am surprised I am not making a fuss that they are trying to microwave a whole chicken… Steve even looks to me for a response, but it is like I am just observing, it's all very funny and we're playing our silly parts again and again with the same outcome, I even tease about some goofy fake fur pants I plan to get my brother-in-law, and my fashionable sister looks at me horrified… Later I am to meet Steve for a trip, he's coming back to the house to pick me up, but my sister needs my car to go to work…and she's dressed in these too big jeans, strange polka dot hose and heels, a vest she made up out of our dead PopPop's pajama top and a nice leather jacket on top of it all. I send her out with my blessing, but need to get my purse out of the car because it has everything I need to go away with Steve. I'm surprised at the floppy little purse that seems so empty (my violet soul purse with a golden clasp)…I never carry purses in my dream…always have what I need somewhere on me… And then I am my daughter meeting her beloved to go to Hawaii.

..and I realize all is superfluous because I must get ready for a wedding...

Then I wake up!

The energy of the dreams was curiosity...taking a trip down the rabbit hole of my subconscious...and at times I try to get out but I know it's all a dream and stay to learn more. There's no fear, just bemusement. I know I am growing while in the dark dream state...I intended this before falling asleep ...I know these dreams represent what I have cleared from my soul purse...my fears of being a woman, my tendencies to get captured by others and taken advantage of, the shame of failing in my healing practice, letting go of the boy to allow room for the divine masculine, being with my family all the interior mothers, fathers, sisters, brothers, daughters, sons and not being smothered by my relationships with them but seeing the humor in life and being gracious with my humanity...then going on the next stage of my soul journey, preparing to experience the sacred marriage of divine feminine and divine masculine within me in the heart of the earth...starting all over again like newlyweds... The last sequence with the empty purse (I never dream of purses!) with Hope not part of the dead but so deeply embedded in my soul, not something to be cleared out of my soul "purse"... something to keep always.

This crazy dream sequence was in fact...the past six months of soul work from the time I planted the seed of intention to be open to receive abundance...through all the work of clearing out all that doesn't serve me, and making room for a great harvest, a filling up of soul...a completeness of self...whole, finally to be whole.

My daughter's wedding, 2014. Jarys (far right) officiated.

17. BLOSSOMING SPIRIT

Every year my women's circle holds a retreat. In 2010, I felt this great need for freedom by the time we chose our theme. The group asked me to intuitively choose a card from the Triple Goddess Deck. I used another woman's Kuan Yin necklace to act as a pendulum. The card chosen was Karmic Imprints and it was all about freedom — freedom from ancestral imprinting and your shadow. The work was deep and dark and powerful. What an amazing life changing retreat. That is where I finally let go of the last of my judgment. Finally let go of Bulimic Deb.

This year before we met for our first planning meeting, crow left me a feather…Bringer of the Triple Goddess Tarot Cards, I tied the triple goddess colors of white, red, and black around the crow feather and the eldest "crone" of our circle used the feather to divine the card. Blossoming Spirit was chosen — card number 5, the hierophant — with a strong rejuvenation theme. Just what I dreamt for our next retreat.

For three weeks, I asked crow for another feather having given up the beautiful one to the circle. And only after I abandoned the search to go on a carefree run with my dog Charlie did I find a black and white feather…balance…and then crow graced me with a pure black feather under the orange tree — where I pick sunshine to consume every morning before greeting my animals and old man crow!

Some of us felt that to truly birth ourselves anew as Blossoming Spirit, we must identify what is golden in the Divine Masculine. Yet most of the circle struggled with patriarchy. The emotional energy was so profound that I can remember to this day who was at the meeting, where they sat, what they wore, what they said. I watched as a few of the women took on the warrior energy while some just left their bodies. I was almost tempted to gather them into a protective circle of white light, when I felt guided to just observe.

After witnessing their reaction, I took my heavy heart to my beloved husband who shone some divine masculine light of wisdom upon me. Then I sat in counsel with my higher self, consulted with wise women and wondered when this Father Wound would be finally healed. For Blossoming Spirit to emerge at the fall equinox, balance must be reached.

It is time to heal the split with the Divine Masculine. I began this work exactly a year ago, composing and publishing two articles regarding the Divine Masculine before I was hit with Death…there my focus lie for months through the Karmic Imprint retreat and well after as I released all that no longer served my soul.

The summer before, I had an amazing dream that reminded me of an aspect of the Divine Masculine that has been forgotten...

I enter the Home Depot through the lumber department to get to the garden center. I'm going to buy jasmine. The center of the Home Depot is a raised platform and as I ascend the steps to the platform, a great Golden Bear comes through the door. It's huge, larger than life, a golden orange color, translucent, brilliantly colored like a child's crayon, surreal. I'm the only one to see it. It snuffles around the entry and I crouch down on the steps. It snuffles its way over to me. And snuffles my hair, my face, my neck. Then taps a great claw over my right eye, then over my third eye, again and again. Then it hunkers down over me like a mother bear over a cub. Yet I know this bear is male. I feel loved and protected like when Steve throws a leg over me, pulls me into his body – trapped by love. Trapped under the bear, I am secure, feeling the soft fur of its belly, the weight of its body, the warmth, the mass...protected in a golden cave of bear energy. Then the bear transforms into a...man. I can feel his naked body, the roughness of his hair, the shift in weight, mass, warmth from bear to man. We stand and face each other. I am WOMAN and He is MAN...all men, naked, dark skin and hair like a Mediterranean man. We take each other's hands and then he disappears. A woman friend of mine says... "That is the forgotten aspect of the Divine Masculine." And I wake up.

When I lie in Steve's arms, his leg pressing over mine — the weight, heat and furriness comfortable, secure, I am very grateful to have found my home in his heart. I live with the Golden Bear energy of the Divine Masculine.

Although I have taken steps to heal my relationship with my own father and it's going well, the Divine Masculine is up again...wanting to be healed in my soul, in the collective feminine, in the world...

18. THE 11:11 PORTALS

Since the beginning of 2011, the 11th of each month has felt...well, different. After the Japanese earthquake, I was sure I wasn't the only one feeling the 11th. So I googled it and found the 11th of each month described as vibrational portals leading to 11-11-11. On 4-11-11, I felt compelled to hold ceremony so I called up Grandmother Kathy and took her to the beach.

In sacred ceremony, we gifted the ocean with the intention of healing the earth. I felt this intense energy coming from the sun...no actually through the sun and recognized the galactic center blessing us. On the wet low tide sands, I danced the sacred union of Father Sun and Mother Earth...what an amazing experience!

Lately, I keep seeing multiples of 11 every time I look at the clock (11, 22, 33, 44). I looked up the significance of these master numbers and calculated my numerology number by birth date and it is 22...but still this doesn't settle my soul...something more is up.

On Monday, I awoke with a vague melancholy. Then I realized the date...7-11-11...and felt compelled to hold ceremony again...but what? Trusting all would be well I opened my journal in hopes of inspiration and.... it came to me...

...These portals are DNA activations! In alignment with the chakra's...the first three were not as noticeable to me (I can only guess that these layers are well activated by Genesis Gold®), the fourth felt like a celebration of the heart chakra...Love... the fifth and sixth were subtle, yet this seventh was in alignment with work I've been doing regarding the Pineal gland. And I have always known the crown chakra to be a connection to the heavens, the multi-dimensional universe. Perhaps why we bow our head in prayer, exposing our crowns to the mouth of God.

So on 7-11-11 at 11:11 dressed in violets, I lay under my oak tree to meditate.

And for the first time since I was a child, I felt the presence of Father God. He spoke to me. Explaining that it took this long for me to bond well with the Divine Mother, to discover my truth and transform from human doing to human being...to live as the embodiment of the Divine Daughter and encompass Divine Mother energy into my life with deep honoring of the Divine Grandmother.

He showed me how easily I partnered with the Divine Masculine in Steve and received it in other men. How bravely I tried to heal my relationship with my father ...yet still I searched for guidance from the Divine Father.

In answer to my heart prayers of healing the father wound, He came.

And showed me, me as light! A juicy brilliant orange-red began the light show and I felt filled from root to belly...hormonally rejuvenated. Then lime green darkening to peridot as the light rose from solar plexus to heart. The greens deepened to a glorious teal, fluid and dancing with lovely lilac in the center…my heart filled. Then my throat alighted in clear blue, brilliant as the sky and here where I hold trepidation, finally healed by the blue light of truth. Then my head filled with violet, not purple of my youth, but a deep violet that circled around to red and became fuchsia. My new auric color! He showed me that I've come full circle and begin again at 50.

The communication was long and deep. For I saw my own DNA dancing. Not the double helix formation but a spiraling spherical star of DNA, many layers deep, no, not layers, He said, not stacked but intertwined, and I looked deeper and saw brilliant strands dancing figure eights of infinity, meeting in the center of the star sphere, some switching partners, some dancing in triplets…Seven lit up brilliantly…four more dancing in the shadows, and the last yet to be enlightened.

All the while Father God spoke to me. He explained how he watched over me all this time through the eyes of crow. My deep connection to this magical black bird that so many fear…it was serving My Father. The one I turned away from so long ago.

No judgment, no sorrow during this glorious reunion with My Father. Only light and love. Exactly what I ask for every time I feel fear. That my fear be lifted and I be filled with light and love. And now I know it has been Him…answering my prayers.

Oh, I am still very much one with My Mother. She flows through me….and I felt Her great Joy as I received Him. She held me in her arms as She presented me, Her Divine Daughter, to My Father. I am so blessed.

I arose at 11:55, 44 minutes in divine communication. I am profoundly affected…the light was so healing…I know now what Yeshua meant by My Father and I are One.

19. IS THE MUSIC STILL PLAYING?

My LoveDance® feels complete…but oh, not yet. It is time to go deeper…time to open the past. I must admit that when I did open my mother's cedar chest, the ghosts of Deborah past knocked me back on my butt. My left sciatic ached for days…birthing pains…time to go back to the beginning. To face the old me. I do not like the way I wrote then…hiding my truth behind too many words…but I shall include some of it…just to see how far I've come on my journey.

Part Three
BIRTHING SELF

20. HOT TUB ADVICE

I'm in the Jacuzzi with Steve enjoying our morning coffee. In the oak sprawled above us, squirrels chatter at crows taking refuge from a pair of bossy jays. This land of ours is teaming with life. Only an acre yet separated into garden rooms so that it feels like three. My mare watches us as the goat rubs against the new gate. The dog pokes his head over the edge of the tub. Steve gives him an affectionate pat. "You know you should start at the end."

"What?" Overhead, a golden hawk cries — messenger of the divine. I listen closely to my beloved.

"Well, I like books that start at the end then go back to how they got there."

"I think that's what is being asked of me…how did I get here?"

He smiles, "I meant for <u>LoveDance</u>®."

I give him a kiss, "Yes, but this is My <u>LoveDance</u>®."

He sighs, "You're going to tell it all, aren't you?"

Yes. Yes I am.

21. HELIUM BALLOON

While this is my story, it's also ours. We've been together since we were kids. Steve's a main character in my story. If it wasn't for him, I may not have reconnected to my truth so early in my life. His love became the foundation of my awakening. He grounds me into this reality so that my dreams might manifest.

When our daughter was only five, she described us as a helium balloon.

"You're the balloon, Mommy."

"Then what's Daddy, Kyra?"

"He's the string!" She rolled her eyes. "Without him, you would fly off to outer space."

After tucking her in with a kiss and a story, I related our conversation to her father.

He laughed. "She's right. I am the string to your balloon. You need me to keep you on earth. And I need you to get me off the ground."

It's sometimes eerie how well we fit together.

When my youngest sister was pregnant with her last child, one of my twin sisters and I gave her baby shower. It was a couple's shower so Steve came along. Exhausted from working a night shift and getting so little sleep before the afternoon shower, he had a headache and went inside to lie down.

I had a great game for the dozen couples to play. It involved diapering a "baby" the old-fashioned way with cloth diapers and pins. The trick was that each couple had to do it together using only one hand. Needless to say, there was a lot of laughter, poorly diapered dolls, and when my pregnant sister and her husband took their turn, a lot of blood and cursing. No one could do it under two minutes.

My other sister had an idea. "Let's see you and Steve do it." I protested. The game was for the guests. "Please," she begged. "I'll get Steve!" And she hurried into the house.

We had never played this silly shower game before but Steve could not resist my sister's pleas. So we linked arms. He was the right hand and I was the left. And silently in perfect unison as if we were one body, we diapered the "baby". My sister held it up, "I knew it! Less than 30 seconds and perfectly diapered. And look, no blood!"

It was so natural to be in perfect harmony with my beloved even for a silly shower game. Like I said, my story is his too.

22. IN THE BEGINNING

So now that I've begun at the end, it's time to go back to the beginning.

In the beginning, there was the One. It just was. No space, no time, no differentiation of any other. Then there was desire. Desire to know itself. Desire to know itself as more. Then there was the Word, the thought expressed. Creation became envisioned. First the One had to understand itself as a Self. The One as Self and then the realization that there are no others. So Self decided to define itself. The concept of space emerged as Self moved its consciousness to the boundaries of Self.

As Self noted that it knew more about its existence then it had in the beginning, time became relevant. Then the One created form. Form as a means to embody space and time. Then the One split into two. The One was like the light and the second aspect of itself was like the dark shadow of the light. Now the One had multiplied with clear differentiation between Itself and the Other. The Light One and the Dark One desired to know themselves as more and began to differentiate into many aspects of Self, each becoming more fragmented from the original One.

Oops...I went a little far back. In 2001, I had this vision, no more like a memory of being One. Like I could remember being part of The One. And then separate. My remembrance of Oneness, I felt whole, holy, complete and then...the separation and I felt less than, incomplete, yearning for more. And in that remembrance, I knew where my sense of unworthiness began. I came in with it and it's been going on for a very long time.

23. PRECIOUS

Yet I've always felt precious. My mother called me her precious daughter until the day she died. My father treats me as if I am a precious gift. My grandparents beheld me with preciousness in their gaze. My aunt and uncle speak of their brief time with me as precious. And I have always felt life is precious. That my relationship with Steve is precious. That my children are precious gifts to me.

So how can preciousness and unworthiness live in one being? Because we live in a dualistic world. We are both self and other. We are both light and dark. We are both divine and human. We are in duality. In duality, we develop our sense of self, our egos. Our ego serves to differentiate us from others. Only when we drop the veil of ego can we be one with all that is. Yet being human, we need differentiation to appreciate connection.

My parents perceived my divine light. And I knew myself as precious until I developed my ego. Then under the veil of ego, I felt separation from all that is and began to feel unworthy. I could no longer perceive my own divine light.

While cleaning a stained-glass lamp, it came to me. The inner light was dull due to the dust of time. Yet polishing the outside of the glass did little to increase the brightness of the light. I had to polish the inside of the glass. Only then did the light shine with its true brilliance.

Same with us. We work so hard polishing our outer selves. Perfecting our appearances, our bodies, our faces, our clothes, the cars we drive, the houses we live in, the people we hang out with, the money in the bank, the roles we play...lots of time polishing our outsides... Never quite good enough always striving for more. Thinner, younger, prettier, stronger, richer, more successful.

Yet until we dive deep within to rediscover our preciousness do we spend time polishing our inner selves. Removing the dust accumulated over the years...the childhood traumas we reflexively relive, the generational thinking we carry as karmic imprints, the old paradigm beliefs we are afraid to give up…until we polish our inner selves does our divine light shine brightly enough for us to see it reflected in the world. In the faces of our family and friends, in our works, in our connection with the earth, in all of our lives.

Steve's graduation from the police academy, 1984. From left to right: Gran, my mother-in-law, Steve, me, Mom, Nana

24. IN THE BATH

As I told my friend, I did not remember my childhood drama until after I gave birth to my first child. Jarys was born ten weeks premature, so we had to wait nearly six weeks before taking him home. Until then he stayed in the NICU at UCLA while Steve worked and I pumped. Day and night around the clock, I pumped my breasts to store the precious milk for our infant. It was all I could do. They wouldn't let us hold him for very long so I spent more time bonding with my pump than my infant. But it was hardly a chore. In spite of the hand pump—I was never offered an electric model to bring home and my experience with the hospital pump was overwhelming—I got very good at using that odd plastic device.

Imagining his tiny face gazing up at me, the smell of the golden down of his head, the clasp of his fingers around my pinky and looking past the tubes riddling his miniscule frame and the antiseptic glow of the hospital, I would feel let down—that incredible fullness released in rhythm with a baby's hunger. My breasts did not differentiate between infants. They let down at the cry of a hungry baby in church, at the grocery store, even on television. My milk seemed to flow for them all. As if through the flow I could somehow connect to my own baby so far away. The sensation of letdown would fill my heart. It's the closest I would get to feeling love. Our bonding was broken by the traumatic delivery and long separation. Only through my imagination could I experience connection. So every few hours, I pumped and feeling a great sense of accomplishment, I would pack up the frozen milk and drive the 90 miles from Goleta to Los Angeles. The nurses teased that I had enough to feed the entire NICU.

My mother lived closer to UCLA so often I would stay with her. Nana was still alive, although dying of metastatic lung cancer. And my youngest sister chose to live with Mom in the tiny condo rather than Dad in our big beautiful home. So it was crowded when I arrived each week after holding vigil besides Jarys' incubator.

One night I awoke from a nightmare. I startled my Mom who was lying on the floor besides the couch. "What is it?" She asked, concerned. I described the dream in vivid detail…

I am four years old carrying the baby and herding the two-year-old twins into the bathroom. After setting the baby in the tub, I lock the door behind us, both doors, the one from the hall and the one leading to our parent's room. Mommy is upset. Daddy is gone. He's always gone. I sing to them and when the baby settles down and the twins begin to play, I call Nana. In my head, I call to her. And soon the phone rings and Mommy answers. It's Nana…I wake up…

Mom confirmed that would happen often. She would be overwhelmed by the care of the four of us and worried about what Dad was doing. What he had been doing at the end of twenty-four-year marriage, not being faithful. They were in the process of getting a divorce when Jarys was born. They didn't tell me right away waiting until I was far enough along in my pregnancy so that I wouldn't miscarry due to the stress. But still it was stressful. We were less than a year married, both starting our careers, expecting a baby and trying to buy a home. Then Nana got sick and my parents announced their divorce, we take in my youngest sister for the summer, as the whole family whirls about in a tornado of change, and I go into labor prematurely. The stress won.

Remembering my past in its fullness not just the fairytale ideal that I had brought into my young adulthood changed me. I knew I didn't want to be like my mother. She felt disempowered by her dependency on my father. I knew I didn't want to be like my grandmother. She lived in a co-dependent relationship with my grandfather who was a recovered alcoholic. I had no other mother figures to model. I had to become a new kind of mom.

My parents' divorce freed my mother. She began speaking her truth. Loudly in a very Italian way, but it was her truth as she knew it. One thing she taught me very early on was how to be in the moment. Jarys was about a year old, cruising around the furniture. I was behind him wiping up his handprints from the glass coffee table when my mother slapped my hand.

"Don't be like me." I looked up surprised. Like my grandmother, my mother was fanatical about cleanliness. I barely remember Nana without a rag in her hand wiping up something and Mom was just like her.

"He'll only be little once. Enjoy it. The dirt doesn't matter." That was the first time I remember maternal advice coming from my mother. I took her words to heart. And I became a more relaxed, in the moment mom, trying not to worry about appearances like how clean my house was, and spent time with my precious child.

When Jarys was twelve I began a deeper level of soul work. I began to clear the dust from the inside of my light shade. I began to write poetry to help heal myself.

I called the collection: Dealing with Feelings through Verse. And through poetry I revisited the bath...

IN THE BATH

the baby is crying

the twins are spying

under the door of the bath

the water is running

she bravely is humming

to drown out her poor mother's wrath

a mere child of four

walked in the bath door

dragging her siblings behind her

a woman emerged,

with so much to hide

childhood lost in a blur

three decades have passed

yet the pain ever lasts

will ever a child she be

or worse even yet

her own children bet

in her, her dear mother they see

she fights with the rage

turning now to the page

to pour out her heart's pain and tears

first kissing her dear ones

then calling up dear mum

to find blessings over all these years

25. EVERLASTING BIRTH PANGS

Late in spring, Steve and I were at Lowes buying veggies for the garden. He left me with a cart full of plants to go get something in the warehouse...a dangerous thing cause I LOVE flowers. Some dahlias called so I knelt to find the one that wanted to come home with me when I was approached by a tiny, slightly bent, very wrinkled, delightfully enthusiastic ancient Native American woman.

"Come, come. You must see these flowers." She beckoned pushing a walker cart. I was enchanted by her energy and followed her. "These are the flowers for you."

She showed me some bright yellow and pink annuals. "Touch them," she insisted. The flowers were dry, perfectly preserved. I was amazed. "Strawflowers!" She exclaimed. "They're for you." I yearned to give her a big hug, but she was so tiny and fragile, I just caressed her shoulder as I thanked her. How could I not buy one?

So I planted a bright yellow strawflower in front and forgot about it...until last Memorial Day. I was on my way to finish my sculpture...and had an uneasy feeling all weekend. Driving over to Grandmother Kathy's house filled with a familiar feeling of anticipation peppered by trepidation, I was transported back to 1984 driving to UCLA to pick up my first born from the NICU, excited but a little scared. My whole life would change when I brought him home. And now my life was changing again.

I cried the moment Kathy hugged me. "What's wrong?" About to bring home another life changing creation, I knew that I would never be the same again.

My sculpture came out of the kiln relatively unscathed (a slight crack in the horse's neck and her left knee...we all have birthmarks and scars, don't we?) The retouch staining went well, but alas Kathy did not have the right glue to attach the crystal amethyst wings to the ceramic back of the woman so off we went to Lowes.

And Kathy led me right over to a lovely display of strawflowers. "Do you know what these are?" I nodded, as a matter of fact I did, and shared the story of the ancient flower woman with her. She was very excited and after getting the glue and another strawflower plant for each of us, we headed back to her house to attach the wings.

As we waited for the glue to dry, Kathy brought out an essential oil...Helichrysum...she said was from strawflower...yet I knew in holding the tiny vial...that wasn't quite right...I envisioned a rougher plant... I was hesitant to smell it...She wondered why and I explained that certain odors are powerful memory inducers for me...finally I did...

...and I was in the tomb anointing Yeshua's hands and feet. Then I went further back to just before the Seder...opening the alabaster jar,

Judas reacted to the scent of the helichrysum...not the spikenard, frankincense or myrrh, but the helichrysum because...it was used to heal wounds, to revive...to resurrect...and now he had to do what was asked of him...he didn't believe and the others, well, they didn't know what was going on...Then I saw myself well before that last Passover collecting tiny dried yellow flowers from a rough lavender looking plant and simmering them in olive oil until the essence was extracted....Tears poured down my cheeks as I remembered...

Kathy was amazed... she called the essence "everlasting" Afterwards I looked it up online (I love my smart phone!) and found the plant from which the oil is derived....it looked like what I envisioned and the Latin name is "Immortelle"...

I found research on helichrysum for use in gingivitis. I decided to try it on my gums...Steve's reaction to the smell was strong...he said it made him feel "very upset... please don't use it again, please" My Mom found it healing, so much so just smelling it relieved a headache... Kathy had the same reaction as Mom...

Now once again I'm astride two worlds...as Jarys would say...the past and the present. Or if there is no time...I'm floating in my river of consciousness between the banks of what was and what will be.

26. RIVER OF CONSCIOUSNESS

My dreams provide clues to my soul growth. How far I've come and what needs to be worked on. I interpret my dreams soulfully — what is my first impression, what feeling do I have about the dream, who were the players in my dream and how do they mirror me? Sometimes I wake up knowing my dream holds great significance — that I've dreamt for human consciousness. I had one of those dreams the summer of 2010...

I enter a house, the one with all the doors, all the rooms, the one I can never find my way out. I've been in the house many times. Always my extended family is there and there is always much chaos. But this time I am not frustrated but move through the house with ease. Just watching, seeing their light, smiling at the comedy, holding the energy. I find my way to the back deck. For the first time, I am outside the house! Below is a creek and I yearn to get in it. So I climb down from the wooden deck and skip down the grassy hillside to the edge of the babbling creek. Then I just lay down in midair and float on the water. It's glorious! The creek sings to me, gently carrying me through the forest. I am enchanted. The view is amazing. Bright topaz sky, brilliant green leaves, rich brown earth kissing the clear water. The energy is palpable. Soon the creek becomes a river wide and rushing. There are people in and out of the water. Most are hanging onto the banks. Some are constructing rafts. They seem so anxious. Children play joyously in the shallows. I float on. Through the rushing river, past rocks, and over waterfalls. Never do I encounter any obstacles. Although many others get banged up in the rapids. The river spills into a swamp and I lie taking in the serenity of still waters. Then past a bog, the current picks up faster and faster until over a waterfall, I spill into the...ocean! I am submerged, surrounded by sea life in the jewel green waters. When I float to the surface, I find chaos – people all around, shipwrecks, airplanes bombing, screaming, crying, and – teens surfing with dolphins, children romping in the surf, sandcastles rising. I emerge from the ocean, like Aphrodite, dressed in goddess white, the sun drying my garments as my feet cross the sand. And there I meet my Higher Self. The golden one with amethyst wings. Her arms open welcoming me home. "Again!" I cry delighted, "I want to do it again!" And she escorts me back to float in the river of consciousness.

Life is a river. Didn't Garth Brooks sing that tune? Funny while I am not a fan of any particular music, I am attracted to soulful lyrics and Mr. Brooks, among a few other artists, sings to my heart. He sings of a vessel that tries to stay between the shores of the river. I believe, this body is our vessel. And the river is consciousness. It wasn't until after I wrote LoveDance® that I understood how we float through life. Some struggle to stay afloat, some build rafts to forge the tide, some just enjoy the water. Now after much soul growth, I gratefully find myself...

Flowing with the river of consciousness, open to the energies, accepting the sweet ripe fruits as they hang lusciously over the waters of life.

Part Four
RELEASING FEAR

27. IMPATIENCE

Last minute doesn't work for me. I am most like the goddess when all my bowls are spinning gracefully in the air. For me, last minute feels as if I'm a clown juggling too many balls knowing they'll soon come tumbling down upon me.

I pack a week ahead. Just be sure I have everything and everything fits. I like to plan ahead for events, ready when the day comes. One of my dearest friends is a Last Minute Lizzie. Every Easter, she would invite us over and twenty more family and friends to celebrate. We would arrive early to help, and find that they were in the midst of a remodeling project (she liked to take advantage of the gathering to get her husband to fix up the house) and she would still need to shop! So off I would go with her while Steve stayed to help him and frantically we would get it together...rarely before the guests arrived...

My sisters like to fly by the seat of their pants too, waiting to shop when we arrive a day or two before the holiday. That can drive me crazy! I need to plan and be ready. After our parents divorced, my home became the gathering place for my three sisters, their spouses and all their children. It was stressful since there was so much to do before they arrived. I wanted to be able to spend time with them, but was usually so wound up by the preparations and wanting everything to be perfect that their visits became more and more of a burden.

No matter how well I was doing at controlling my eating disorder, the stress of the holidays would bring Bulimic Deb out of her cage. I yearned for quiet holidays. The more stressed I got, the more I would find myself counseling patients with the same Superwoman Syndrome. I would tell them — just say No! — yet could not take my own advice. Finally, after ten years of this holiday madness, I told one of my sisters I couldn't do it anymore. It was their turn to play Mom.

Yet it wasn't where we met that made me so anxious. It was being in their energy. I could tolerate my friend's frenetic energy, but not my sisters. We were too close and would fall into the roles we always played from the drama of our childhood. The more I found peace in my own life, the more frenetic their energy felt. I couldn't seem to stay centered when I was in their midst.

Every gathering there would be blow up. I was always looking for their souls and they were hiding behind our roles.

Nov 28th, 2004

Finally a breakthrough with my sisters! Always I have dreaded our family gatherings. Early in my adult life, I fretted over the work related to the holidays, then feelings of unworthiness as I worried about the outcome. Was everything good enough? Was I? Lately dealing with deep seated emotion that threatens to boil over, I have not shared my life with my sisters fearing that we could not find common grounds to safely communicate. Still there are gaps but we are closer after this weekend's tumultuous confrontation, all four of us crying in the bathroom. We needed a red tent and had to create our own chamam experience. Our passion brought on spooky weather. Bitter rain, harsh winds targeted the house. Our husbands took the kids to the mall where the weather was nicer. My sisters claimed that I did not share all with them and I replied that I feared to reveal to them the true fullness of my emotion—my power can be overwhelming. They pushed, then got blown away, then came back for more. My sisters are hardier than I thought. I do feel loved by them but do not believe I appreciate them fully. My sisters are aspects of the divine. They say I feel superior, but I see their unhappiness, their fear, their unwillingness, it seems, to progress. Yet I realize that just because I have leapt so far away from what was our mutual starting point does not mean that they have not also moved. Steve has kept pace, and in their own way, so have they.

As a point being I am supported by their effort, faith, and love. Without them would I be where I am in this moment? I am buoyed up by their beingness, my own being reflected in the stillness of theirs, in the wake of their progress, exponential reflections of our conscious evolution. Why must we name our faults and weaknesses to equalize the interaction? Yet I do it when I counsel with patients, admitting my humanness, and we grow together.

Over the years I've learned to flow more easily when things don't always fall into place. Now I graciously step into my friend's house and just lend a hand. And she too has learned to get it together earlier and enjoy her guests.

For my 50th birthday, my sisters treated me to a weekend away. I prefer being in nature so we took a boat trip out to Anacapa

Island. No drama just pleasant memories of picnicking on the bluff in the midst of nesting seagulls. My sisters still want to know where I am coming from…I have changed so much. On a beach walk, one expressed concern that she thought I felt our family was dysfunctional. I smiled…three of us had eating disorders, all of us grew up with disordered body images, our mother still struggled with self-esteem and our father lived like a hermit… "I guess every family is somewhat dysfunctional," I replied.

Then the conversation became confrontational and for the first time in six months, I felt that need to purge. I placed my hand on my stomach and watched as my sister expanded into warrior pose, then I was cast back into our childhood dining room feeling the fear bubbling up as she argued vehemently with our father—always fighting another's battle—and ending up in trouble herself. And I came back to the present and spoke my truth.

"Thank you for embodying the warrior in our family. But I am not the enemy. I am your sister and I love you." And since then, there has been peace.

It took me 50 years to flow even with my family. How strange it feels to not care about the outcome, but to be fully in the moment with them. I can get used to this. ☺

28. FAMILY TIES

Learning to be my truth within my family of origin has taken a very long time. It is our soul work to witness our lessons in the mirror of those we love. And families are magnifying lenses…

Dec 23rd, 2003

Off to Utah for the family holidays. Anxious premonitions of my beloved Santa cup breaking. After 20 years of keeping them safe for my sisters, I tried to pack them carefully, but one tumbled out of the car, so I traded my unscathed cup for the fractured one. This trip is about breaking attachments, perhaps to things, but yet deeper, to what I believed my sisters to be. As I am coming to know myself as joyous passion I shall recognize who they are as love. So many sister dreams lately. Since childhood, I have flown in my dreams stringing them along like Peter Pan, barely able to get them off the ground. Lately in my dreams, I do not hold their hands, but try to teach them to fly on their own, but they resist. I feel tired, saddened. Will my sisters throw me out like Yeshua was thrown out of Nazareth? Strangers can be more accepting than those closest when you change too rapidly.

Dec 26th, 2003

A snowstorm traps us in the house, playing games, memories abound. On Christmas Eve, I experienced the power of the loving-kindness prayer. The family gathered around my sister's large kitchen island arguing about the Cody Bank's rape charge. When the manner in which the victim dressed was blamed, I felt the urge to jump into the fray, yet stopped and silently asked that my fear be lifted and I be filled with light and love, then asked the same for each and every one of them. When I got to Kyra, she looked up and mouthed, "What are you doing?"

"Blessing us," I silently replied. The tension melted. The brothers-in-law about to engage in fist a cuffs, laughed at another's joke and all was well. This morning my youngest sister hugged me fiercely claiming she thinks about me every day. Lately I can say the same. I wish I could see beyond the possessive love in this family, the competitiveness, the criticism, the ego...especially mine—my ego is much too overwhelming. My muse is on holiday, but lots of purple around me, my aura brilliant whenever I close my eyes. Torn between gluttony and deprivation, defenseless in the face of my family without bulimia to protect me. Trapped in a house of mirrors. One: reflecting unforgiving close-mindedness, one: emotional, temperamental, quick to strike, yet a core of love, one: distant, shallow immersion, non-committal, one: lost in a world of self, one: poor self-esteem, critical of all, not knowing when to hold her tongue, my brothers-in-law, my nieces and nephews clueless bystanders, my husband supportive, policing my behavior. This journal my only escape...

29. LIFTING THE VEIL OF FEAR

When Mary Magdalen's story came to me, it was overwhelming. I felt a little psychotic with the multidimensional experiences yet enchanted by the fluid reception of divine guidance. Just three months earlier, my former mentor and I were having lunch and as usual, before we could just sit back and chat, guidance came in for me—through her. "You need to reconnect, Deb!"

My mentor knew it was time to cut the cord. So she moved. Just like that and I was alone. Or so I thought.

So I set my intentions to have my own connection. And two weeks later dreamt I was Mary Magdalen. Receiving HerStory in such an amazing fashion seemed an answer to my prayers. I sought validation for my interdimensional experiences by confiding in women old enough to be my mother. Women who had claimed their sixth sense, some even making a living by working with the energies. While they supported my creative process, I could not see that I was searching for the Divine Mother through them rather than find the connection in my own heart. With my horas nature, I bared my soul and shared everything with them.

From the moment I dreamt I was Mary Magdalen dancing down the streets of Nazareth, I was in constant contact with the other side…and it wasn't just voices, it was a full body experience. It was so profound that some of my more sensitive patients reacted to the change in me. One clairvoyant asked, "Who's your entourage?" Mostly it was Yeshua, angelic beings, and sometimes my ancestors…much later I understood that I separated the divine aspects of me from my human self. I know now they are all me.

Sept 17th, 2003

Overwhelmed, giddy from the experience of writing the first chapter, I felt like I was not revealing a memory but living in the moment. I could smell the odors, see the colors and textures, feel the wind, the linen, the touch of his hand. I am being transformed and once again as I sit here to type, the front door blows in, the wind chimes sing, the birds chitter rapidly. A presence is here again which guides me.

Sept 18th, 2003

What a revelation—on my son's nineteenth birthday no less! I awoke to liquid purple teardrops slipping through my consciousness. The purple is what I see when I meditate and lately has been calling me to be still. This time I associated the purple with Yeshua and we talked like lovers, old friends, companions. I am clearer now on the multidimensional nature of reality. Yeshua described how he can be here with me as Deborah incarnate on this earth, and alive and well in my past life memory. It is all NOW. There is no time. The entity of Jesus Christ was not the man—Yeshua. "You must present us as the human beings we were, I was a man first." I asked why he doesn't come in like this to comfort me, like with my suffering over finances. He said I could be so silly, that the security situation was being taken care of, as Steve pointed out, always grounding me. I got the immediate vision that my husband was Teoma. Steve had taken many lifetimes to be with me in this way, always before protecting the bloodline. Then Yeshua spoke fondly of my daughter, "Kyra is so beautiful, I miss her."

Sept 19th, 2003

So much comes in with Yeshua more deeply entwined in my life. Sometimes we are merged, most of the time we hold very human conversations, and more often his energetic presence is bordering on the physical. I feel rushed, excited, frustrated. The rest of the historical details coming in pieces, I strove for clarity in a text book all the while getting more confused as the dates seemed wrong. I could hear Yeshua advising me to put it down and just write. It's so interesting that when I relax, the verse just flows in present tense, all my senses are attuned to the writing as I taste, smell, feel the experience. As I become more distracted and nervous about the content, I distance myself unconsciously by writing in the past tense.

I have always been open to that which is unseen, unheard, unfelt by others. Although traditionally trained as a family nurse practitioner and in spite of post graduate courses in molecular biology, quantum physics, neuro-immune-endocrinology, functional genetics and integrative medicine, I trust my intuition to guide me. It is my innate ability to perceive the root cause of dis-ease that patients seek.

Bridging the gap between the physical and the spiritual, the energy and the matter, I made profound insights into health and wellbeing. My colleagues and patients enthusiastically encouraged me to write a healing book. In the summer of 2003, I struggled to compose a self-help manual, but nothing. So I prayed to be shown a way…and it came in a dream.

My dream babies, Halloween 1988

I believe in dreams. I dreamt of my children before conceiving them. I dreamt of the house we live in now. Even my nutritional formula, Genesis Gold®, came to me via dreams. The first one in Aramaic! Was I being prepared to receive a forgotten story?

One of the most profound lessons came very early. Just six days after the dream of Mary...

Sept 22nd, 2003

Just before dusk on the vernal equinox I was literally shown–experienced in body– how fear interferes with the connection. What went from a 24/7 experience in the emotion of gratitude, love, joy, delight, desire was absolutely cutoff by sheer panic while riding my high strung mare. Although hesitant I trusted Yeshua's guidance but when Shane became spooked at something in the field, I perceived what felt like a divine set up. Yeshua kept coming in and out, advising me to massage acupuncture points on her ears, to walk slowly, to breathe consciously, but terrified, Shane bolted.

Unable to control her, I literally screamed for Yeshua, but it was as if we were cut off, barely making contact, like a radio station going in and out. Shane's half ton of equine terror greatly magnified my fear. Even after I dismounted, she nearly trampled me. Shaking with anger, feeling abandoned, betrayed, the fear of separation from all I know was at the heart of my despair. Finally I began singing to calm us both — a lullaby I sang to the kids — "Do you know where you're going? Do you know where you've been..." and through the song I answered the proverbial questions (why am I here, what is my purpose?)

I was shown that in my childhood I had constant connection. I remember speaking to G-D, but as I got older, I felt unsupported by the world and vanquished my emerging womanhood through anorexia. Somehow I believed that once I came into my feminine power, my mission would begin. How many years did I take the masculine stance in a world where only fierce competitors survived, imparting my intelligence, my strength, my courage, my leadership, but sacrificing the fullness of the sacred feminine. My fear cut off the divine connection then and now.

Slowly settling, neck arched, head tucked into me as if I could protect her, Shane no longer trembled and snorted. Just before Yeshua finally slipped fully back into my consciousness I realized that the low vibration of fear had prevented me from connecting to his higher vibration. Only fear veils us from the Divine.

106

Which was profound since the next day, I had to go to court for the very first time. And I was scared.

Thank goodness in twenty years of delivering health care, I have never been to court, but the day after this amazing reconnection, I was subpoenaed as an expert witness. Appearing in court brought up so much anxiety that I wished it away. And the case had been postponed for over a year, yet the time had come to face my fear. In order to become an expert witness, you must first undergo voir dire—a process in which lawyers determine your competence as an expert witness—but it's more like being crucified.

Fully connected to the vibration of love, the protective energies so powerful around me that in spite of the defense lawyer's tortuous questioning to make me appear incompetent, the judge looked at me and said, "God help me, but I am going to qualify you."

Afterwards, the prosecuting attorney, also an author, asked how my book was coming along. When I excitedly told him how effortlessly the words flowed from my visions onto the computer, he exclaimed, "Sounds like you found the holy grail!"

Yes, I did.

For eight moon cycles I recorded Mary Magdalen's life—in the first person, present tense—as if I had lived it. All the while, reading each precious piece to the mothers in my life. Of course they loved it; their "daughter" was creating something wonderful. Some were fearful for me as they peered into the future expecting this controversial book to upend my existence. Others lived vicariously through Mary, amazed as I wrote dramatic experiences of womanhood, some of which I have not lived, yet they confirmed the truth of the telling. Many of my presale readers asked if this story reflected my life and were surprised when I denied specific events for it seemed so real. Perhaps I tapped into a vein of consciousness that allowed me to flow into another's life, experience her very breath, and return to this reality to record every sensation.

Shane and me, 2010

30. THE GRANDMOTHERS COUNCIL

After Divine Mother was healed, Divine Daughter was Unveiled through the writing of <u>LoveDance</u>®. I made peace with the Divine Mother energies, received the Divine Mother within myself, learned to mother me and birthed myself as the Divine Daughter. I then published my first book in November 2007 and began 2008 ready to begin book two of the <u>LoveDance</u>® trilogy and was stymied...

It began with the Grandmother's Council. Just after <u>LoveDance</u>® was released, a jolly lady showed up in my office wanting to buy a book. Delighted I signed it for her. She gazed at the cover and said, "The grandmothers would love to know more about the divine daughter energy."

"The grandmothers?"

"Yes, the Grandmother's Council of Ojai. Would you come and speak to our group?"

Of course! They met the second Sunday of every month so when my schedule freed up from marketing my book, I went to the Grandmothers Council to share the Divine Daughter with them. They received me joyously and then preceded to offer empowerments. I watched and was transported back to Mary's time once again.

These gracious older women surrounded those who came to them in a veil of love, placed healing hands upon them and blessed them. Tears poured from my eyes as I watched the ancient rites delivered with such love in these modern times.

Then the head grandmother turned to me and asked, "Don't you want an empowerment?"

I thought I was there to present…not to receive…yet…I nodded, "Yes, please." And stood within their loving embrace as the grandmothers veiled me so I might just receive, placed tender hands upon me and began to sing.

"Oh, how we love you. Oh, how we love you…"

And the ancestors came in…all the matriarchal lineage in a beam of light. The spirits guided me through the great grandmother saying they are very proud of me and the work I am doing, that they are always here for me, pushing, nudging whispering encouragement. Now is not the time to stand still. Now is the time to be in the world.

It was profound. And the grandmothers have been with me in spirit and in body ever since.

31. LIFE HAPPENS

By the summer of 2008, I got reconnected to my old way of communicating with spirit. Something I called conversations with God as a kid transformed that summer into Q&A. I got a brand-new journal and dedicated it to conversations with my higher self and began on July 11th 2008 my divine Q&A...

Q: What do I release?
A: Your fear

I didn't like that answer, so I asked the question differently...

Q: What do I sacrifice in my life to make room for abundance?
A: Your Fear

Hmm. My Higher Self was being evasive...

Q: What am I afraid of?
A: Not being good enough to complete your mission
Not being your truth
Not returning home
Being alone — separated

Leaving behind what you love…

Q: I must release all this??
A: Just the fear. The rest will fall into place. Have faith — easy for you. Do not be discouraged by others nor by life. All obstacles are tests that strengthen your character. Ask for help — you are surrounded by those willing to be of assistance if you but ask. Don't push them away with your fear.

Wow! She really knew me!

Q: So much I know, but am not yet. When will I be?
A: You are complete — yihidra

Still no practical answers. Seems like spirit communicates in riddles. Same with my old gurus, not much was given in clear steps, but rather comfort in general. I tried again…

Q: Ok, so what human step must I take right now?
A: Be Joy. Love All. When the time is ripe you shall receive the full rich harvest.

Q: So the time is not yet right?
A: Ripe.

Q: Ripe?

A: The fall is the time to harvest.

Q: Hmm. What now?

A: Enjoy the time you have with your loved ones.

Q: But I love too much…

A: Not possible. You do take on too much. Others are not your responsibility. Free will is theirs. You are here to enlighten with the model of your life, your being. They may not wake up. They may not follow. They may choose darkness. Let them go…

And from then on, I was reconnected with my higher self.

Many more questions were answered. Yet the most unique aspect of this journaling my conversations with my Higher Self were the reflections upon looking at insights given in the past and living the present circumstance. For the Divine, there is no Time. Only the human me defines herself by the past, the present and the future, yet all exist in the Now.

My higher-self identified herself as …I am You. Divinely connected. Remembering all that was, all that is, all that will be.

I am Timeless. You are me in earthbound form. I am you in heavenly connection.

32. STRUGGLING TO LET GO

At the same time, I reconnected to my Higher Self, I had completed a struggle to get my book rights back from the publisher. Although I was so grateful to have my book published, I expected much more than they delivered. Like printing enough copies so Amazon would not run out before the holidays. My contract included the "opportunity" to purchase a short run of a thousand books at wholesale to sell directly at my presentations. And after I purchased my books, their support ended. Another soul lesson unfolded...

Q: My sorrow at dismissing my publishing partner to go out on my own magnifies everyone I've left behind.
A: Do not lie paralyzed by grief. Rise up from the mire of your doubt.

Q: What do I doubt?

A: Yourself. Your greatness. Your abilities as a co-creator. Your divinity.

Q: No, I know I am Divine...

A: You have little "gnosis". Because you push away your Divinity, keep it at bay — for you fear being rejected.

Q: It feels as if I'm already being rejected

A: Divinity shines through you! I AM Here. Just Ask and You shall Receive...

Q: So what is my next step?

A: This fear has to be released fully. What you have been vomiting up, what creates anxiety, what separates you from that which you love. It must be fully released.

Let go of all that does not serve you, that doesn't bring you joy.

Q: I wish to release my fear but how?

A: In quiet moments, be still and open your chakras — Red to Violet — a prism of white light will encompass you. Into this portal let your fear pass.

Q: I feel hesitant

A: You have held on for so long

Q: Will it be fully gone?

A: Yes, but molecular memory will take longer to forgive

Q: Forgive, not forget?

A: Gratitude for your humanity, forgive yourself for choosing fear over love.

So I asked to see my fear. And every one of my fears manifested. I faced, I embraced and had the time of my life. I had gnosis through Joyous Service. And abundance began to pour in…while the rest of the nation lived in recession, I lived in transformation. The abundance came as enough money to fill our needs, as opportunities to grow, as family to know better, all interwoven.

I manifest as I type. What I write becomes…

33. KNOWING THE ALL

Recently I began to check out channeling that has been going on for 22 years. Benevolent guidance from the other side through a man who in this life is an engineer. My engineer brother-in-law would scoff as I'm sure this man did when he first received interdimensional communication. I believe women are more open, the feminine being naturally receptive.

I am in awe of the confirmation of what I know…revealed to me at the same time and sometimes before it was channeled through those who openly share the guidance they receive. I guess knowing they are out there makes it easier for me to come out of the closet and share what I know.

A month after I reconnected to my higher self, I wrote…

Q: Tomorrow I have been married 25 years!
A: Millenniums together from time eternal, playing different parts of creation. Yeshua watches as your love blossoms into its fullness with great hope for the future of this planet. Your love becomes the portal in which Divine Mother Earth may pass through to the 4th-5th-6th dimensions. Three petals, three

118

dimensions unfolding in triads. It is time for the Earth and its inhabitants to pass into the next universe, soon so soon

Q: 2012?
A: Yes, 2013 will be its birth, its delivery after a long 2012 transition. Really since Kyra's conception in 1987 the birth pangs began — labor — she labors — you labor to deliver her. The rest of consciousness, the mass awakenings are souls who wish to progress. The rest will stay behind in darkness — the dream of their making.

Q: I thought no soul left behind?
A: You cannot save them all. Each has free will to stay or to go. You can only show the way. That is your frustration. Your fatigue is from holding the energies — being the way — for those who cannot see, those who pay no attention. You can only create small openings and the light will shine through. They may not receive the light of love. You did enough — move on and Be The Way!

Patience is not one of my best virtues. So waiting has been hard. Just Being rather than Doing goes against everything we are taught. Yet it is The Way. To Be the Light of Love. And I "know" and now have "gnosis" that is gets easier. As the vibration of the planet rises, we may resonate or not. Those who do feel the ease and avert dis-ease.

34. FEAR TRANSFORMED INTO JOY

So now fresh from my reconnection with my higher self, I set my intentions to see the face of my fears. The time was ripe. And the universe presented the fruits of my labors.

In late August 2008, I got an urgent call. My mother-in-law was being taken by ambulance from Santa Maria to Santa Barbara. And she wanted me. Before she allowed the doctors to do anything, she wanted me there. I am her medical agent, the one responsible for following her end of life wishes, yet she was fully cognizant, just scared.

So I drove the 45 miles to the hospital knowing this was it. I would be facing one of my fears. As a nurse practitioner, I had been called upon by the family many times over the years for medical advice. It was assumed by my elders that I would be the one to take care of them. And frankly, after decades of providing care for others I did not want to end my life as a caretaker. Plus being a caretaker is hard physically, mentally and emotionally. I have counseled many suffering from depression, insomnia, anxiety, and utter exhaustion from long spans of care-taking.

I knew that it was time to take in Steve's grandmother while his mother recuperated. And then we would take her. And I knew my husband would agree to whatever I decided and would do everything he could to help. And I also knew it would be me doing all the work.

So I stepped into the ER and stepped into my fear. The family gratefully released all to me. My mother-in-law only signed the emergency surgery release after I counseled with her. It was clear that Steve's grandmother was not happy being handed over to his aunt and uncle. So once his mother was taken to the operating room, we offered to take Gran. There was little resistance.

Gran came home with us. She was delight, but not safe with her rickety cane on our hard wood floors. So we got her a four wheel drive walker and at 89 years old Gran became mobile again. My mother-in-law had been living with her for the past six years and slowly Gran lost her ability to be productive...or so we thought. To me she was more than willing, so I put her to work. Gran was delighted to help and we found her much more capable than her daughters had reported.

She helped fold clothes while watching Ellen every afternoon and in the evening helped me with dinner. When Steve finally brought his mother home from the hospital, she was surprised to see Gran cutting veggies. "She can't use a knife! She's on Coumadin!"

I smiled. "She's been very careful and if she cuts herself, luckily I can stitch her up."

Shortly after she arrived, Gran said, "Since my stroke, I can't smell very well. So you'll have to tell me if I need a bath." A day or two later, I sniffed her and announced it was time. She balked a bit nervous to have me help her in and out of the bath. But I had the perfect set up. Our guest bath had a tiny soaking tub with a seat inside an enclosed shower. So I warmed up the bath, and helped her in. Then she sat down, "Uh, oh!"

"What?"

"You aren't going to be able to get me up." The seat was too low and her arthritic knees were higher than her hips.

122

"It's ok, Gran. I'm a nurse. I know how to lift you."

She shook her head, "You're too little."

"I'm strong, Gran, and Steve's here if we need help…"

"Oh, no. I don't want Stevie to help." Great!

Ten minutes later, all parts of Gran were sparkling clean and I was soaked. After a failed attempt to lift her from the edge of the tub. I stripped off my sodden nightgown and climbed in with her. She laughed telling me that's how her other daughter did it. I placed one knee between hers, squatted down, "one, two, three" and lifted Gran to her feet. She held me tight as I helped her over the edge of the tub and she didn't let me go.

"It's so nice to hold you like this," she whispered. It was nice. "But there's only three breasts between us!" She had had a mastectomy thirteen years before. I almost dropped her laughing!

That was Gran always finding delight in everything. I know it's not easy accepting help especially if your role in life is to be of service. I hope I am a gracious patient and not a burden on my loved ones. But the stress of illness and the demeaning role of incapacitation can make the best of us turn sour. Yet Gran was a delight.

My mother-in-law was another story. I have yet to meet a medical professional who is a good let alone gracious patient and my mother-in-law is a retired nurse. She also had become one of those resentful caretakers that I didn't want to emulate. So although my care-taking load more than doubled when Steve brought her home from the hospital, I was determined not to lose myself and took time every day for me.

Shortly after they arrived I got a call from Steve's cousin. She had just been diagnosed with breast cancer. When it rains it does pour. So I spent time counseling her, helping her to see the spiritual message of the dis-ease. I find that breast cancer patients are very good at taking care of others, but quite poor at self-care. Their body speaks to them through the dis-ease. "Time to nurse me please." I think she got it. And so did I.

I was so busy during this time, that I did not record it. There is nearly a month missing in my journals yet it is burnt into my memory. And it happened again the very next year. And the second time, I took care of them both for months instead of weeks. Yet in spite of the incredible stress, I am left with such pleasant memories.

Every afternoon, after Ellen, Gran asked if I was free to have coffee with her. I was still seeing patients three days a week in my office which is on our property. My mother ran my practice and was in charge of keeping an eye on Gran while I was in with a patient. Gran would push her walker out onto the patio overlooking the herb garden and chat with the patients as they admired the flowers. And when the last one left, I would sit and have a cup of coffee with her.

And I learned how to sit and enjoy being. Gran loved the garden, the flowers, the hummingbirds that would visit us, the butterflies, even the jays that shooed the songbirds from the feeders and especially the antics of the squirrels as they scolded the cat and the crows. Gran took delight in being alive. And I took delight in being with her.

My fear of care-taking transformed into joyous service. I had written about joyous service in LoveDance® but for the first time, I got to experience it. The family thought I was a saint. My husband cannot thank me enough. Yet it was I who am ever grateful for the opportunity to serve in love and joy.

Part Five
BOXING SPIRITUALITY

35. DO YOU PRACTICE WICCA?

My friend is at it again. She called with yet another probing question. "Do you practice Wicca?"

Hmm. I wasn't sure what to say. "I wouldn't call my "practice" Wiccan. I hate to put my spirituality into a box."

She clarified, "Well, I passed your book onto my daughter and she wondered about the symbol on the cover. It is a pentagram, isn't it?"

Technically, yes. The star in the rose is five pointed. It came to me in a vision. I learned later that the pentagram was used by Wiccans. But to me it is sacred geometry. Mathematical proportions and symbols are very attractive to me. The energy of form speaks to my soul.

Back to Wicca. Years ago my husband was part of a police investigation. Some blood found in a park, ashes from fires set in geometric patterns. Before pursuing criminal charges, he felt strongly that what they were investigating was the residual of a pagan ritual. So he did his own investigation. And sure enough, he was right. And then stood up to protect the suspects' right to freedom of religion under the Constitution.

Now it helped that he was friends with a young Wiccan. Not that he knew much about pagan practices. So she lent him a book — a Wiccan primer. And after studying it, he announced, "We might be pagan, Deb."

Really? We had been spending our Sabbath in nature for years. Teaching our children reverence for the earth, the trees, the rocks, the animals. We quietly celebrated the changing of the seasons…sending out holiday greetings to our friends of many different faiths…on the winter solstice. My spring equinox birthday naturally lent to celebration and the fall equinox corresponded with our son's birth. On the summer solstice, we welcomed the hot long days of summer.

Nature was our church. Our temple grounds — the earth under our feet. The canopy of trees our cathedrals. We were nature based in our spirituality. We buried our pets with special reverence. We held communion with the ocean, dipped our feet in her healing waters, and thanked the powers that be for our bountiful life.

Yet we followed no particular religious dogma...not Wicca. Perhaps more Native American. Although we respect the great masters like the Buddha and Jesus Christ, we have no rules. Must spirituality be boxed in to be defined?

36. THIS IS NOT MY GOD

In the summer of 2002 as our son prepared for college, our daughter prepared to enter high school. She had some heavy reading assignments for her honors English class. Fortunately, our son was an avid reader of the classics so we had the books she needed. One on Greek and Roman mythology and the other, a King James version of the Bible.

And Jarys had read them both as well the Wiccan handbook, books on Native American spirituality, books on Buddhism,

Islam and Judaism, interpretations of the Dead Sea Scrolls, well, pretty much all the theological books in our library.

Unlike her brother, Kyra was not much of a reader, but she had no trouble with the mythology. Yet halfway through the book of Genesis, she stated, "This is not my God!"

"What do you mean?" I asked, serving dinner.

"The god in this book is a very mean and judgmental god. I like the Greek gods better."

Jarys tried to explain that the reason her teacher had assigned this reading material is that these works have greatly influenced western civilization.

"No one believes in the Greek and Roman gods anymore, but who believes in this god?" She held up the bible.

"Christians and the part you're reading is also in the Jewish scriptures." Her brother explained. "Just think of it as a story book. At the end of the Christian version, there's a tragic hero."

"What happens?"

"He's killed."

Now she was getting upset. "That's how this ends? I hate stories with sad endings.

"Oh, there's a sequel. He's supposed to come back and save all the people who believe in him."

"Come back. You mean reincarnated?"

Jarys laughed. "Oh no, there's no reincarnation in that book. That's Buddhism and Hinduism."

She shook her head sadly, "I don't get it. Why are there so many religions?"

"Because there are so many different cultures and each has a different way to explain life and death."

She nodded. "You're going to make a good teacher, Jarys."

"Thanks." He said and buried himself in a book.

Jarys and me at Stonehenge, 2013

37. BEING MORMON

Yes, I was Mormon as a teenager. And yes, we were married in the Mormon temple. And my friend's family was Mormon. And one of my sisters is still Mormon.

Being Mormon was my idea. It least that's how I remember it. Going into high school was difficult enough, but having to watch over my sisters, well, that was nearly impossible. The only church at the time with an active youth group was Mormon. And they preached no alcohol, no drugs, no sex before marriage. Great! If I could figure out how to get my sisters into that Mormon youth group, well, they would be a better influence than the influence of the sex, drugs and rock and roll crowd.

So I invited the Mormon missionaries to the house. It was a no-brainer. They were handsome young men in suits. My sisters were 11 and 13 and very fond of handsome young men. And one was IN LOVE with Donny Osmond. Her side of the room was purple and plastered with the teen idol. Like I said...a no-brainer.

And we were baptized. Me, my three sisters, and my mother. My father thought we were nuts. He hadn't succumbed to the Catholic pressure and now we were switching teams. My mother joined to keep an eye on us. Well, she didn't just join, she kind of took over. Led the young woman's group...really, kept her eye on us.

And it worked! No one got pregnant before marriage. No one got in trouble with drugs or alcohol and not with the law. And I no longer had to be the shepherdess of my sisters. Thank goodness.

Now being a good student, I took Mormonism seriously at the time. I read the book of Mormon, their Doctrines and Covenants, and the bible (for the first time, since Catholics don't have bibles, at least we didn't).

The good thing about being Mormon was the sisterhood. The bad thing was the patriarchy.

I had the same issue with Mormonism as I had with Catholicism. I needed no man to intervene on my behalf. Why couldn't women hold the priesthood? At that time, black men couldn't hold the priesthood either. Which wasn't fair in my eyes, rather prejudice, I felt. I'm not sure why, something to do with Jesus being white…but I knew that was wrong…cause in spite of their pictures…Jesus was brown, way darker than any of us. At least the Jesus who had been visiting me since I was little was really dark.

Oh, and another thing about Mormonism. I didn't believe in the whole save yourself for marriage thing. I saved myself for my soul mate. Once I found him, well, we were sixteen and seventeen, spilling over with hormones, and we loved each other. I was saved...by love. My torturer was anorexia and reconnecting to love saved me. Thank God for Steve!

But I still wanted to get married in the temple. Why? Because I liked the idea of being sealed for eternity. It seemed like we had searched forever to find each other. Perhaps a sacred marriage ceremony would insure we wouldn't get separated again.

So Steve joined the Mormon church. As he says, "I wanted you. And would do anything to make you happy.' And that's what I thought would make you happy at the time.

The church felt like we had community. And then we moved away. But being Mormon meant instant community wherever you are. So we found a stake center. That's what Mormons call the place they meet. Mormon temples are for sacred ceremonies like marriages and baptisms for the dead. Yes, the dead are baptized and then married. That's why the Mormons are so into genealogy...to find their ancestors and seal them all into one great big Mormon heaven. Now that's how I remember being Mormon.

38. LEAVING THE CHURCH

Judgment made me leave the church. It happened about nine years after baptism. I was in grad school, commuting to UCLA three days a week for class and to work the weekend night shifts at the medical center. Steve was a police officer for the city of Santa Barbara. We lived in Ventura. We didn't get to see much of each other…working opposite shifts to be home with our two-year-old son.

I asked my husband how he felt about my becoming a nurse practitioner. With a master's degree as an advanced practice nurse, I would be out earning him. And our school counselors had been counseling the grad students on the possibility of marital instability. Steve wasn't very communicative then.

It was stressful. We had been together for eight years…never having explored any other possibilities…just following my plan. College, marriage, house, baby…in that order. Now grad school,

136

a career shift, then another baby…too planned. Too idealistic. My fairytale life needed to get a reality check. Right before the semester started I knew we needed a break.

So we agreed to keep our son at the condo. I would stay with Steve's Gran who lived closer to UCLA when he was with Jarys and he would rent a room in Santa Barbara when I was with Jarys. Because of our shift work, we still needed childcare. The next morning, I brought Jarys to the sitter — a nice lady from the Mormon church who ran a home daycare. When I announced the change in our schedules, she promptly handed my son back to me. "I won't be party to adultery."

I was shocked. Granted I had taken off my wedding ring and we had agreed that whatever happened during this "break" would be a learning experience for both of us. But we hadn't done anything yet. I asked if she could recommend anyone else to watch my son. She couldn't recommend anyone outside of the church.

That was it. My last moment of being Mormon. Without the church to depend on, then what?

Feeling very much lost, I took Jarys with me to class. He was very good. My professors were understanding. And thankfully, his great grandmother was delighted to have him. When Steve needed to work, my father was the one we depended on. He had just moved to Ventura. We were back to depending on family. And Jarys. Well, he still remembers those great times he spent with his grandparents!

39. IN THE BEGINNING I WAS CATHOLIC

I was born Roman Catholic. My mother is full blooded Italian. My father is Heinz 57 — a blend of English, Irish, Welsh, and maybe a little African because us girls got our bottoms from somewhere more exotic. And there is that old photo of my great-great-great grandparents with seven or eight children and one is black. Who knows?

So we were Catholic. Well, all except Dad. He wasn't anything of the religious persuasion. Dad believes in what is right in front of him. Not a spiritual person, but his doubt allowed me at least to be open to other possibilities. He wonders why I am so different than my sisters. I believe it was a combination of my mother's faith and his doubt.

Mom and Dad eloped in March of 1960. She thought she was pregnant with me. She wasn't. I came the next year. She feels she cheated herself out of a big Italian wedding, but she did get Dad to the local priest. And he took lessons so they could be married in the church. By that time she WAS pregnant with me—very, very pregnant. She tells the story that the priest liked to imbibe and in his drunken state whispered to Dad that he didn't have to go through with this to which Mom exclaimed, "Father, I'm the Catholic!"

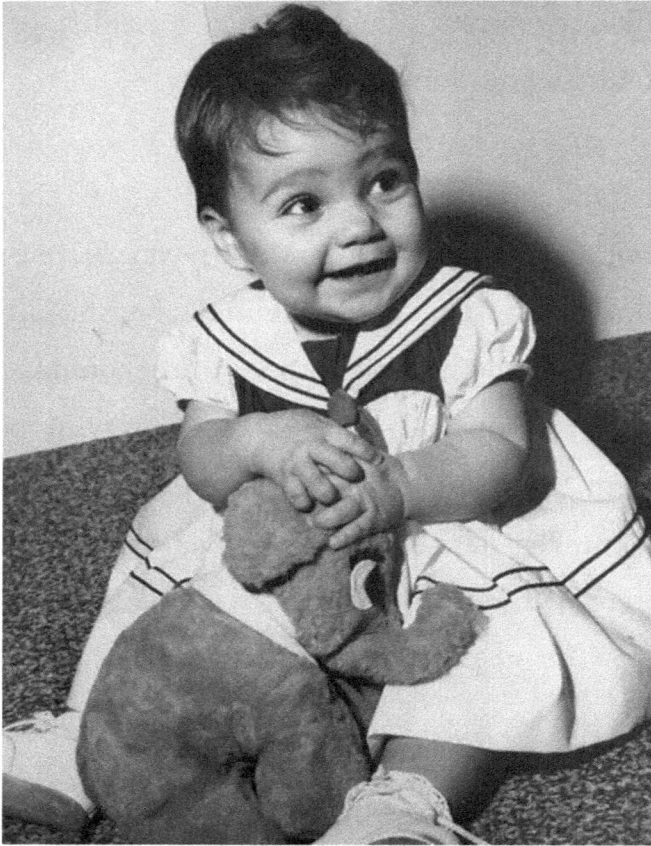

Philadelphia, 1961

So we were all duly christened. I still have my tiny christening gown. And I went to catechism. I loved school, so the classes were nice enough. The church was very pretty. Our Lady of Perpetual Help. A lovely statue of the Virgin Mary all dressed in light blue graced the church. She was very pretty and her baby — Jesus — was very sweet. I loved dressing up in my frilly frocks, hats and gloves and on special holidays, I had a little purse. And

140

every mass, we would get up and down and up and down while the priest chanted in Latin, and then there would be a special moment when all the adults and the big kids got up and reverently made their way to the front of the church and then the priest would give them a cookie!

I really wanted to be part of the church. And you had to learn about being Catholic in order to partake in holy communion. That's what they called the cookie. I found out later it was a wafer-thin cracker that tasted like sour grape juice and stuck to roof of your mouth if you tried to talk which was why you had to be quiet.

The nuns were very strict. And they didn't like me asking questions.

"Why do I need to be bad in order to talk to the priest?" I was having trouble figuring out what I was going to confess.

"Why does the priest have to talk to God for me?" I talked to God directly and He talked to me. And the one they called His Son, well, he was my playmate.

But in order to partake in your first communion, you had to go to confession, which meant you had to tell the priest something you did wrong. I wracked my little brain for something. Then right before my first confession, I did it. I was bad. I gave my little sister less than half of the cookie I had saved from Brownies. I did it on purpose which is a greater sin, but I had to tell that priest something!

Finally, I got to receive holy communion. And Mommy was so happy and my grandparents made such a fuss. And then I don't remember going to church too often after that. Just Easter and Christmas.

It was because of Dad. He didn't like us to be away so long every Sunday. That was his day with us and he wasn't going to share us with God. By the time, we were teenagers, he wasn't so possessive as long as church didn't interfere with dinner and especially Monday night football. Which was a bit of a problem for us as Mormons because Monday night is Family Home Evening and it's hard to have lessons with the TV blaring. It was harder on us to be Mormon than Catholic. It's not just because Catholics understand football. It's because Mormons feel sorry for a family without the priesthood in the house. And Dad wasn't joining!

Mom was a joiner. She loved community in any form and the Catholic Church provided community for its parishioners. And when we could no longer go to mass easily (we moved even farther from church when I was in sixth grade) the Mormon church provided the community she desired. Plus she wasn't letting her daughters alone with those darn missionaries — law of chastity or not!

40. A HERETIC IN THE VATICAN

And then I dreamt I was Mary Magdalen. And ten days later we were in Rome. Oh, not because the archdiocese found out about my visions…because it was our 20th anniversary trip to Italy.

Our first European trip was right after 911…but that's another story. Maybe later ☺…

We began in Rome and on the second day visited the Vatican. Imagine this. Me — educated in scientific theorem, left brained, mathematical, logical, yet trusting my intuition implicitly with a lifetime of prophetic dreams — ascending the winding staircase leading to the Sistine Chapel. The energy of the art overwhelms me. Emotion drips from the frescos. I can hardly breathe. A guard takes notice and gently guides me to an open window. I take gasping breaths of fresh air. "Not everyone is so sensitive." He nods towards the herd of people peering at the art like they are visiting the zoo. Apparently not.

Torn between visions of the past and the present hustle and bustle of this iconic museum, I realize viscerally how the sacred feminine was lost. I knew...yet didn't have gnosis of this loss until I walked the ancient streets with my husband in form and Yeshua in spirit. Behind a covey of nuns, I say silently. "They believe they're married to you." And I hear, *Not Yeshua the man, but the mythical Christ.*

Before entering St Peter's square, I hesitate. Yeshua's presence is so palpable even Steve perceives it. "Come on, you two! I bought the tickets and we are going in!"

It costs a little to view history...the religious relics...It cost a lot to be reminded of a past not completely told. And to have HerStory flooding my memory.

Grateful to openly discuss my visions with Steve, yet feeling a little schizophrenic with the aliveness of this other reality...the voices, the images, the feelings, I am in between the worlds. Yeshua, angels, facets of god…brought more vividly to life in the ancient city.

September 27, 2003

In the wee morning hours I am awakened from a dream in which I as Deborah am laying my hands on Mary Magdalen who is laying her hands on me blessing one another as goddesses unto eternity. Then all energies merge into one essence. I lay face down on the bed flattened out by the sheer power of the dream with Yeshua comforting me, whispering, I am she, I am the goddess. I know the secret of manifestation, I know joy. I am joy as is the hummingbird. I taste all of the nectar in life.

Then as I turn onto my back, my hands clasped in prayer, I am guided by the angel Gabriel, who I recognize as the one who escorted me as Mary into my womb to share the forgotten secrets of womanhood. Then Archangel Michael speaks from my right, reminded me that I also have been escorted from darkness by Archangel Lucifer (known as Uriel in Hebrew or God's light) who smiles at me from my left and delivers me back to myself, back to the One. Then I feel Angel Raphael as the muse behind me fueling my spirit, challenging me to reveal myself to the world. Yeshua speaks, then I hear for the first time the Father above me, the Mother on my left, Yeshua at my right hand as I am his left.

The Father speaks- I am beloved, he has never forsaken me, I will remember all but for now I am to live in the eternal now blending past and present into a glorious future. I can see the glory of my relationship with Steve, as my beloved husband, and Kyra with her joyful goddess energy as a reflection of my own, and Jarys coming into the world manifesting a blend of masculine and feminine energies as an experiment to know himself as god. All my worries are lifted. I am asked to open my heart and to open my arms and invite in abundance. I am reassured that I will be and have been protected and held in the bosom of the One, for I am the joy and he/she/it/the beloved is well pleased.

I breathe in Yeshua, the son, the lover, my friend, and the Mother and the Father. I am whole and I am holy. I am asked to release from my heart all that I believe have forsaken me, then bless them with peace, love, joy and comfort, re-invite them back as whole and accept the abundance and forgiveness for myself and for all. I am freed from all bonds. Even my bulimia is revealed unto me as the false judgment of self not deserving love or abundance. Since the 16th it has been over. I am free and this trip is to be enjoyed with Steve in the eternal Now.

Time is not a line but a spiral circling back and forth weaving in and out of the now. My Italian experience removed layers of history, revealing to me my own truth. I knew for the first time myself as an embodiment of the goddess. Growing up with the patriarchal judgment I saw mirrored in the world, I used the son energies of reasoning and academia to survive as I spent most of my early life being the scientist, exploring the masculine aspect of self, at 42 I found myself being born again as a sacred feminine embodiment of emotion, my power lies in the creative energies as I manifest beauty and love in my life. Finally, I was free to be the divine daughter filled with passion, emotion and love, infused in relationship to all that is, with people, plants, animals, angels, souls past and present. A bridge to reunite the mind, body, spirit with Love.

September 29, 2003
More comes in clearly during the emotional experience of exploring the museums. The renaissance and mediaeval buildings are enough to inspire a passionate awakening. The art pulls at my heart strings. The depictions of Christ as a mythical

being rather than a man. I just feel that they got it wrong! Yet who am I to enlighten them

While in Italy, I dreamt of attending a conference where I share with a huge audience how to become consciously connected by highlighting exactly what happened to me. I realized that I would someday share my revelation with the world, yet the novel came first and changed my writing style increasing my interdimensional connections creating such an awakening that I would no longer write academically but intimately.

October 7, 2003

My life will be written from my perspective now as well as my life as Mary. Which is fact and which is fiction? They are both my realities

41. FIGHTING OVER GOD

At my Mormon sister's daughter's wedding a few years ago, my aunt (a Buddhist married to a protestant minister) asked how the church responded to my book. She had read LoveDance® and loved it.

"Oh, we're not part of the church anymore. Gosh, not for the past 22 years!"

"Well, that makes sense. I wondered where you got your material."

"I dreamt it and later researched what I wrote." I shared with her that a few months after I wrote a particularly disturbing part regarding the Essenes in Qumran (it disturbed me because I knew what the Dead Sea scholars thought they found and what I "saw" and wrote was very different), my rabbi friend called me up to tell me archeologist had just discovered evidence of what I wrote.

Apparently, when one of us remembers the past it opens the doorway for the truth to be discovered. It's like how inventors are often working on the same inventions at the same time. Archeologists are always surprised to find modern technology in ancient ruins. I believe it's because we think we're the only ones. The only ones who know the truth.

Which is why so many religions believe that their way is the only way to get to heaven. And why there are so many jokes about who you'll find in heaven. And why there are so many wars.

When we were in the Vatican, Steve said "Wars are seeded in religious conflict". Including, I think, the Church of the Golden Coins. Because most wars bring the victors much wealth. Except the last one...

911 was the beginning of the end for many of us. The moment the towers were hit, I felt it. Although I didn't know until my mother called a few minutes later what had happened. I couldn't tell her what I felt. Nor anyone for a very long time. But I felt...great relief.

Like finally the birth waters had burst. The pressure was on. Time to push. It felt like the birth of the New Earth was finally eminent and that was such a great relief. Everyone was frantic of course. We hooked up our cable just to be a part of the tragedy. For days, we watched with the rest of the world. Finally, my daughter said enough. "Let's turn it off, Mommy. We aren't helping them by watching. Maybe we should send white light?" I heartily agreed.

Something happened to us on September 11th 2001. I wrote this poem the day after...

The Commencement

After all the tragedy, how will we react

Will we sit in fear, anticipating

Or will we allow the opening of our hearts

Letting this event move us beyond

Dear ones just on the other side of the veil

Watching us, wondering if their sacrifice be in vain

Will we face the challenge with love

Or will we lash out in fear

We have reached the fork in the road

Which path will humanity choose

As the leader of the free world

They are looking to us to choose wisely

No longer the time of Solomon,

Although biblical tales true for then

Yet an eye for an eye, a warrior's cry

Be not the best choice for our souls' sake

We are our own enemy

Not good against evil

But a gracious opportunity

To find a way to heal

Dark and light are both of the One

Let go of judgment, let go of fear

Live in love and enjoy this life

Live in fear and repeat the cycle

React as the male warrior

And we take a step back

React with feminine compassion

And we move into the next dimension

It's time to change, it's time to love

Release the United States and be a United World

Una faza, una raza, one face, one race

For we are each a facet of the One

Even those who appear to be dark players

On the stage of life, we cannot all be heroes

Some of us offered to play the villains

So the rest could learn about love

Thank the players, wish them well,

Our karmic cycles to end

If we release fear, once and for all

Never again will we have to play dark parts

911 was an emergency call

A call to arms, not weapons

But a linking of arms, a holding of hands

Uniting us in a circle of love

Joined together as one being,

No one richer, no one poorer

Children living with conscious adults

Free from fear, surrounded by love

It's time to make our choice

Choose to evolve the collective human soul

To be in a higher dimension of awareness

Embrace the commencement of the age of compassion

Perhaps I was ten years before my time. That is not unusual for me. But I do see a shift in our reality. I see hope. I see change. I see that we have evolved. This last war (and I pray it is our last!) brought us transformation. And that's better than gold.

When only one of us realizes our light, we illuminate our world. That is my hope. That by shining my light into your world, you find your own divine light. It matters not what you call your god…for all is of the One…and it is all Divine.

42. BACK AGAIN

And I write this now while sitting in the cool cave-like basement of my sister's house in Utah. I am taking refuge from the heat of the kitchen. Literally, it's hot at 8:30 in the morning in mid-September. Mom started cooking meatballs as soon as the sun was up. Yes, meatballs. We're having a baby shower. Doesn't everyone have meatballs at a shower?

And it's figuratively hot up there. My sisters and I are so different. They hate honey. I love honey. They ask me to make granola while I'm here. But it requires honey. They concede. And vanilla and cinnamon and ginger…

"Oh, no ginger!" They say.

"But you liked my granola" enough to ask me to make it again, "and I make it with ginger."

"We liked the first batch you gave us, that last batch was too much."

Hmmm. And I say aloud, "That's interesting, cause my family liked that batch the best."

"We're your family!"

"I mean the family I created."

And I come downstairs to take refuge in my writing as I have done since I was a girl.

My sisters are much closer to one another than I am to any of them. I've tried over the years. I should be with them now shopping, (which I hate…to shop…not them) bonding, yet it is not my way. Really has never been. Besides it's that Last Minute Lizzie thing. Although I must admit every gathering is a bit better. They seem more prepared or perhaps I am more tolerant.

My memories and theirs are not the same. We witnessed our lives so differently. And they have taken refuge in each other so their memories have merged. I am learning to love them where they are now. Even if I do not get a voice. That's why they do not know me and probably I do not know them very well. Trying to separate one from the pack is hard. So when we get together I am lost.

They attend well to one another yet not to me. True we don't have much in common. They read all the same books. They listen to the same music. They all watch TV. And that's what they like to talk about...the fiction, the rock stars, the reality shows. I can't keep up.

So our bonding over the years has come in the form of crisis...I'm good with helping others in need. So they come for support and I try to offer wisdom, some of which they receive. And then I do not hear from them until the next crisis or family gathering, whatever comes first.

This gathering is my fault. I wanted, truly wanted, to honor my niece who is having the first baby. I said nothing, but if I want it enough, it becomes. So I was not surprised shortly after voicing my desire to Steve, I get a call from my sister. She wants to surprise her daughter with a baby shower and would like for me to come. So here I am.

Wondering how they will feel about me telling my story…

Do we really choose the family we're born into? I do believe so…to learn soul lessons. Mine has taught me tolerance. And how to be my truth in the midst of chaos…I'm still working on this one. Because family of origin brings up your deepest darkest soul issues. Goddess, bless them.

They're home now…I can hear their pounding footsteps above me and their loud voices…sounds like arguing but it's not. It's family that loves so hard to bruise. When it comes down to what's important…our family gathers…and cooks and eats, and sticks together because blood is thicker than water. But that's Italian…isn't it?

Besides the sauce is off. Remember the meatballs? There's no wine. It's my Mormon sister's daughter who's having a baby. Oh, and Mom couldn't find oregano That's ok. My sister takes me out to her garden… "Isn't this oregano" Yep. I snip some off and take it into the hot kitchen to help fix the sauce that will smother the meatballs that the guests will enjoy in honor of my niece. She's having a baby! And maybe I can get some time alone with her and offer a sacred feminine blessing. I think she'll like that...

43. CAUSE WE'RE ITALIAN

A few days before Steve's Gran died, she was expressing her gratitude: "I'm so fortunate to have my family taking care of me." My mother-in-law responded, "Of course, Mom, it's what families do." Gran smiled, "It's because we're Italian."

My mother-in-law gently explained that they are not Italian. (In fact very Anglo-Saxon. The family name is Jones!) Now I'm from an Italian American family and Gran spent an awful lot of time with us...I do believe Italian rubbed off on her. How could it not? We spent most of the time in the kitchen cooking. The rest of the time in the garden enjoying a cup of coffee. Gran loved her coffee. While she was here, I never drank so much in my life! "Come, Debbie, have a cup of coffee with me." She would ask late in the afternoon. "Oh, and maybe we can have those cookies we made the other day. Just a couple. We don't want to spoil our dinner." How could I refuse? It was precious time spent with an amazing woman...my only grandma.

Italians pass the time playing cards. Gran never played cards before, but she learned fast. Her youngest daughter was surprised, "Mother doesn't play cards!" Gran was brought up in the Reformed Church of the Latter Day Saints...no card playing allowed, no dancing, no drinking, no swearing. Well, in our house Gran played Gin-Rummy, enjoyed "just a sip" of Steve's homemade wine and no, not a virgin margarita, but a real one "you know I love the salted rim!" and once we were having a frank discussion after dinner about the consequences of proposition 8 and Gran got upset, "It's no one's damn business who people love!" Oh yes, and she and I would dance. Foregoing the walker, I would hold her tightly in my arms and we'd sway to the music.

When Kyra would come home, we would all be in the kitchen making something delicious. My Mom would join us—she runs my practice which is right here on our property so I could be home for the kids and then for Gran—four generations making fig jam, stuffing zucchinis, preparing yet another meal. Mom would squeeze Gran and give her a kiss. "It's not a kitchen without a grandma in it!" Just as Gran took me in as her granddaughter, she treated my mother as a daughter.

Gran had enough love for all of us and more. Years ago, she "adopted" a young black man who reveres her. And her Hispanic caretaker came to the hospital in February, laid her head next to Gran's and wept. She stayed hours petting and fussing over Gran.

Gran worked in the Farmers Market for thirty something years making friends with Jewish, Asian, Hispanic and Blacks. She did not see race or color or religion or sexual preference. Gran only saw people. And she was always delighted to meet them, all of them...and perhaps share a cup of coffee?

Steve and I were reminiscing. I know you tend to elevate the dead, forgetting their worldly transgressions and focusing on the good. But no need to embellish Gran. Like Steve said, "She was always genuinely glad to see me, she accepted me completely and my presence brought her joy." Gran treated all of us like this...in her presence our truth shone...because she really "saw" us...she looked past the shadows and embraced the light in each of us...

Steve believes karma is incurred over your lifetime. He's spent his consciously banking good karma. Gran didn't know much about karma...but her bank was full. I believe karma can be imprinted. My research shows it begins in the womb...remember the Red Cord...yet I have been branded by Gran. She has imprinted me to the roots of my soul.

When the family made plans for the funeral, I called my mother-in-law and told her "Mom said the Italian side of the family is cooking! Oh, and we don't do petit fours." She laughed and told her sister. I could hear Auntie in the background. "Thank goodness, I love tomato, mozzarella and basil."

I've entitled the menu—Gran's Day—the day we gathered to celebrate her life: Bruschetta, melon and prosciutto, marinated grilled veggies, olives, of course lots of bread to dip in Mom's sauce...she's doing most of the cooking. I'm the baker in the family... Gran loved my holiday cookies and they go so very well with a cup of coffee.

Mom comes up behind me and gives me a hug and a kiss on the back of my neck, "Someday you'll do this for me."

There are no tears as we connect in the kitchen—Gran joins us—to reminisce and to prepare delicious food, lots of it… It's what family does…because we're Italian.

Part Six
SEARCHING FOR SELF

44. CIRCLES OF SISTERS

I am sitting in a circle with my mother, my sisters, and my nieces. In the center lies a deck of Druid Animal Oracles. With a bit of Irish and a tad of Scottish blood running through our veins, our interest is piqued. A few summers before I had introduced my sisters to Medicine Cards from the Native American tradition. These cards represent the animals sacred to the Celtic tradition. Time to reconnect to our roots.

We each pick five cards. Each of us uses a different method to choose yet all choose wisely. The cards seem to speak to our souls. The center represents Self. The East is Intellect. The South is Sensuality. The West is Emotion. The North is Intuition. The cards come with a book interpreting each oracle. "Let Aunt Debbie read. It sounds more real when she reads." My youngest niece scribes while I read.

While my eldest niece attends closely, the rest have trouble giving their full attention to the one whose turn it is to choose. We could use a talking stick. Over the years, I have noticed how little we attend to each other. We each have something funnier or more brilliant to contribute than what is being spoken in the moment. Crosstalk is rampant at every gathering. If you cannot attend to everything going on at once then you get lost. Perry Sister brilliance is loud and quick…few can keep up with us.

In my women's circle, we pass the talking "stick" or crystal or feather and each woman has a turn to share what's going on in her life. The rest of us attend quietly only giving insight if she asks. After sharing at the last circle, we needed to discuss the retreat schedule. These ethereal women don't do business. So it got chaotic…few understood what was needed, women were offering random suggestions and the one trying to keep notes got lost. My Perry Sister brilliance clicked on as I interpreted all the crosstalk. The note taker asked how I was able to do it. "I listen fast." I replied.

Yet as I watched my nieces try to understand the meaning of their cards, I witnessed my sisters chat amongst themselves not really present in the moment. It was interesting how many cards in common we all had…but we are family. My youngest sister and I both chose Goose and like Mother Goose, we are very maternal. I share Seal with my sister, the mother of my four nieces. Seal represents True Love, Longing and Dilemma. I've been faced with many dilemmas in my life and longed to know myself as love. I've found True Love.

We are at a time of our lives when The Change can force change upon us. Grandchildren come to us just as our fertility leaves us. Our spouses are changing too, sometimes for the better, sometimes not fast enough. We long for something. Many menopausal women begin their spiritual journeys. That's one of the gifts of being Hormonally Challenged. You begin to see your life through different eyes…and you want more.

My husband told me once in the midst of my searching. "You climb up the fence to get to the grass on the other side and at the top you meet someone climbing over to get to your grass." He says it's all the same grass…perceived through different eyes.

True. But we all go through times when we need to be sure our grass is as green as it gets.

46. SACRED FEMININE CONNECTIONS

I alone chose Cat as the Druid oracle of my Intuition. Cat is aware of the spirit world. That I am. Cat observes without judgment. This, I'll have to work on.

In 2003, I was given the Medicine Cards as a gift and promptly chose my nine animal totems. Was I shocked! I had thought of myself as strong almost masculine in my ability to achieve. Yet I chose very feminine cards. Even my masculine side was represented by Spider which the Native Americans refer to as Grandmother Spider, the one who weaves our reality.

And Steve chose very masculine cards like Wolf and Mountain Lion. While I showed the world my tough side, Steve had no qualms revealing his softer side. The friend who gifted me with the cards was not surprised by my totems. "The world perceives you as very feminine, in spite of your masculine stance."

The veil had been lifted. And from then on I knew myself as an embodiment of the Sacred Feminine. Writing LoveDance® allowed me to live freely as Woman. As the Divine Daughter, I danced my heart through the free expression of my emotion.

166

And over time, I have come to cherish my Divine Mother Self. Now entering menopause, I hope to know myself as the Divine Grandmother.

The Change doesn't come quickly. It is a process. I recognized this after reading <u>Women Who Run With the Wolves</u>.

April 5, 2009

I am undergoing a transformation. I am entering the change...and it is truly changing my life. My relationship with my sisters is improved. And although I rarely write, rarely blog, rarely market, all the old seeds are coming to fruit.

Dreams are lucid, exploring my inner psyche. I am being initiated into the grandmother's council and I love it.

I type this on a new computer. The old died, like so much passing in my life...Sara, Auntie, Karen ...death leads to birth. The winds of change clear the way for the new.

Most profound of all is my ability to instantly manifest. What I think becomes. If I desire something greatly enough, it manifests. I have had little need to confront my worries as they absolve before me. I am in the state of realization. Becoming the Magdalen, the way to the divine.

The polarity of good and evil does not exist in my world. All is of joy. All is of love. All is well. Lessons cloaked in distasteful garb are often the most profound. Rarely is it difficult now. I move into my sage-hood with ease.

Estes relates stories as a means to understand the psyche. I see great connection with LoveDance® and her rendition of the archetypal stories. I naturally wrote into the story the maiden, the child-self, the queen/bride, the king/groom, the mage and the gardener. Perhaps this is why the book touches so many on such a deep level. Story heals souls.

I am so very well, so very blessed. Gratitude has become a way of life. Love is my essence. The world is opening to receive me and I am prepared to bare all to be Joy.

And here in this book, I bare all and you, my reader, are open to receive. Tonight I shall take the role of Crone in the triad that serves our women's circle. A practice run as sage or the beginning of the next phase of my life…hmmm…

47. MEDICINE WHEELS AND SACRED SPACES

Like many on their journey, I turned to the writing of others to learn more about myself. In the 90's I was fascinated by Native American spirituality and read most of Mary Summer Rain's books in which she is mentored by a Native American elder…a grandmother of great wisdom. I am grateful the author shared her path. So much so that I share mine with you now.

So I created a Medicine Wheel garden in our side yard. I divided the eight sections with rocks and planted each section with the same types of flowers and herbs. In each I placed sacred items representing my path on the medicine wheel. And the garden grew so lovely, except in those areas that I needed to work on — self-esteem and relationships. Another message from Mother Earth to me.

When we moved here I longed for another Medicine Wheel. We created garden spaces, beautiful outdoor rooms lush with plants. The herb garden, my patients pass through to get to the office, grew lush and vibrant in less than six weeks. My husband and I have very green thumbs. I plant intuitively and he puts in the watering and keeps the critters under control. Well, he and the cat keep the critters under control.

In the north section of our property is our horse corral. The barn was built shortly after the house in the 50's, so there's horse energy in the place of wisdom. Though I find my horse most wise indeed, I still envisioned a Medicine Wheel under the sprawling oak in the north corner. There I would seek wisdom from the land, from Gaia herself.

We had perfect rocks for the Medicine Wheel. Dug up by the pool builders, these smooth golden boulders would mark the directions elegantly. But Steve had parked the horse trailer under the oak. How I longed for another Medicine Wheel…

And one day, the oak split and crushed the trailer that was parked in the spot designated for my Medicine Wheel. That's what I get for wanting something badly enough. It comes to me. I don't miss the horse trailer, but I sure do love my Medicine Wheel. And so does my horse ☺

Shane treats the Medicine Wheel as sacred, at least she seems to. I never find manure within the circle. The old gelding that died last fall wasn't as respectful. Yet a few years ago, we were watching the Fourth of July firework display when the horses spooked and ran into the circle of rocks, then turned and calmly watched the fireworks with us.

In the morning after I feed and pick up manure, I seek refuge in my Medicine Wheel. I sit on the Eastern rock and meditate. Usually the animals join me. Fortunately, the rock is big enough for me, a cat in my lap, a dog by my side and a pygmy goat. The horse doesn't try to get into my lap like the goat, but she hovers. It's awesome to be surrounded by my beloved animals.

It's important for my soul growth to create sacred spaces. I recommend it to my patients when they begin their journey or are feeling lost. Create a sacred space. Somewhere in your home or outside in the garden, set aside a spot for you to connect to your Higher Self. Outside I have my Medicine Wheel. Inside I have My Altar.

48. MY ALTAR, MYSELF

Directly across from the door to our home is my altar. A lavender macramé cloth covers the small winged table. Objects sacred to me adorn the four corners with candles in the cardinal directions.

The altar changes from time to time according to my needs. Often my children ask to be put on the altar. And I make elaborate altars for them, holding the energy as they face challenges like when my son interviewed for his first real teaching job (and thankfully got it!) and my daughter tested for nursing school (and she got in too!) When Steve's Gran first fell ill, he asked me to dedicate an altar for her. And after she passed, the altar reflected our love and devotion to her.

Today, items sacred to our upcoming retreat lie on the altar…The red cord I made to help us connect to our ancestors and each other. The crow's feather bound in triple goddess colors that helped us choose the theme of our retreat. A golden frame filled with photos of men I treasure—my husband, my son, my father, my grandfather—my beloved divine masculine.

And in the front—my Box of Me. I made this one up…but what healing has come from creating a Box of Me. It started just after my father's surgery, my sisters had moved him into a senior apartment complex and found a box of old photos. In it was a photo I do not recall, but looking at the black and white image of me at thirteen months old dressed in an Easter dress holding a little purse and gazing out with old soul eyes, I remembered. Showing my parents how to parent me and feeling their emotions. I took that photo and pasted it on the Box of Me. Somehow I would heal the child within. And through the Box of Me, placing me on my altar.

Inside the Box of Me, the mementos change yet each represents my dreams, my hopes, my intentions. I've guided many patients and some women friends in the creation of a Box of Me. How therapeutic it has been to honor ourselves, to put into this special box all that we hope for and say to the universe YES! Yes, I am. And more so to fall in love with ourselves. Because that's where love starts. If we don't love and honor and cherish ourselves, how can we love and honor and cherish each other?

It's hard for most women to make a Box of Me…harder yet to place anything sacred within their Box of Me. It is a start, a fresh start to healing the child within. I ask them to choose a photo of themselves that is before the time they remember the trauma of childhood. The innocent time before becoming domesticated into humanity. A time when they remember being happy. Few go back to adolescence, most go back to early childhood, some all the way back to infancy.

In the center lies the golden runner embroidered by Steve's Yia Yia...a wedding gift given to me by his father who came from Greece to witness our union 28 years ago. Upon the runner sits Ascension.

49. ASCENSION

During a guided meditation in my women's circle, I saw an image of my Higher Self. Emerging from the heart of the earth, I sat astride a powerful horse, my golden body in sweet repose, a heavy dampness on my back...furled wings! Feeling compelled to create Her into form, I took my joy to my Q&A journal where I converse with my Higher Self. I'm the Q, she's the A...

Q. Your form amazed me!
A. I am your Higher Self. Well connected to the Mother with the ability to fly through the dimensions.

Q. I would love to paint you, but I have not the skill

A. Ahh. You will see that your ability to manifest is not limited to what you know but all you "remember". Time is a spiral. There is an artist in you.

I prefer to work with my hands so I thought "maybe a sculpture". So I called Grandmother Kathy. She's a retired art teacher. I asked if she had clay I could come and play with. "Of course!" she said and every Monday morning for 13 weeks I went to her house.

Grandmother Kathy midwifed me as I birthed my vision. The process was amazing. I never before created anything with such ease. I would work a little and then just put it aside. Patience was also birthed from my play with clay.

My Higher-Self assured me that my hands would "remember" how to form clay. And they did...

Ascension

This sculpture that I created—I call Her, Ascension—is my Higher Self formed from clay. Not only feminine, but in sacred union with the masculine. That is who I am now. She is who I've become in my 50 years on earth. Finally balanced.

When She was ready to be taken out of the kiln I drove to Kathy's house filled with trepidation...and remembered for the first time...the feeling of driving to UCLA to pick up Jarys from the NICU. My whole life was going to change when I brought HER home, just like it did when I brought Jarys home. Not that I hadn't transitioned in the time it took to create HER or the time it took to gestate, birth and wait for my premature baby to be strong enough to come home. Then I was cast back to 1984…my life forever changed by Jarys' birth…

I nearly died giving birth. I had a rare form of toxemia called HEELP syndrome in which my sky rocketing blood pressure caused seizures while my liver and kidneys started to fail. And our premature 2 ½ pound baby was born intersex. While pregnant, I dreamt of a blond baby boy, so it was no surprise when our baby's chromosome test revealed the male XY pattern. Yet the pediatric endocrinologist advised we raise our child as a girl. Neither of our mothers understood. The doctor explained that our child would not have secondary sex characteristics.

"What's that?" Our mothers asked. So I explained. "Body and facial hair."

They laughed. "We're Greek and Italian. The women in our family have to shave! That's no reason to castrate the baby!" The endocrinologist had no experience with families who did not follow her medical advice. We were told, "It's easier to make a hole than a pole." I was shocked, not by the bluntness, but by the total lack of consideration for the effect of "his" hormones on the developing brain. If we raised "him" as a girl what psychological trauma would "she" undergo at puberty or later in young adulthood. The experts didn't know. So at 22 and 23 years old, Steve and I had to make a very difficult choice. We decided to follow my intuition, go against medical advice, and raise our baby as a boy.

Finally bring Jarys home, 1984

Jarys became my impetus to learn everything about hormones. I felt intuitively that his DNA was not set in stone but could change. He could make cell receptors for male hormone. He

178

could be anything he wanted to be. So I became a hormone expert which led to developing an Intuitive Integrative Medical model, which led to researching the hypothalamus and genetic upregulation, which led to the dreams of a formula to optimize genetic potential, which led to the manufacture of Genesis Gold®…which has changed my life…

Since bringing Ascension home, my life has changed again. My relationship has deepened even more with my beloved husband. My relationship with my mother became more refined. I have truly released my son and he is blossoming. My daughter grows in leaps and bounds and no longer am I entangled with her. My relationship with my sisters is blooming…no drama at the last family gathering. And being with my father was joyous…Thank God! I am in deep gratitude to my Higher Self for helping me birth my truth.

50. COMING HOME

I did not leave to find myself. Although Steve may say otherwise. The Mary experience was something else. Truly I was in between the worlds. Often he would ask me where I was when we took a walk and I would fall silent. I was in Galilee during those times. He felt me slip, how could he not?

So yes, for the eight months I composed my novel, I was barely here. In body, if not in spirit. I vowed not to do it again like that. Perhaps that's why book two took so long to write. But I think it's more likely that I cannot write what I do not know and I am just now coming into realization of my power as a creator of my reality...that there's nowhere to go to find the truth...but within.

Many women and men leave everything they know to seek enlightenment. It just seems too darn hard to find peace and truth in the midst of the chaos of your life. Yet I did it. Many of us have stayed and found enlightenment right at home, within our communities, serving our neighbors, raising our families, walking the dogs. There's nowhere to go. Heaven's right there on earth ☺

March 5, 2003

The One came and it was joyous. Beginning with laughter and ending in laughter. Lightness as a child. I felt free and happy and maintain that joyousness even now. I shared it with another right away so I could say the meditation to ground it into my being. After nearly two hours the most significant piece surfaced back into my memory. God's strategic plan for life is within the DNA.

I began my meditation with questions of truth and untruth. What are my misperceptions? The One came in a bubble of glee, laughing at my seriousness for it is not my nature. *You are the funny one, the one that laughs freely, you are my joy. This meditation is not your way. It is for those serious sages that seek to commune with me.* The One was all joy, all bliss.

Do you come to those serious ones who meditate with this same delight? *Of course. I come to all who ask, as I am them and they are me.*

I come to them in the form they can appreciate, stifling my laughter as not to offend. With you, I can laugh freely for you are lightness and joy. But you came to me when I began this serious meditation? *Because I had to laugh at you. I am always with you. You recognize me through the glasses of your choosing. You, my dear, are choosing laughter and delight. Within your delight, your joy, your wonder, I exist. I am the joy, the light, the laughter, the bliss. And I am you.*

The One came and I asked are you the mother or the brother? It claimed to be all of them and everything and nothing. It is me and the world, the universe. It explained that life is like a spiral of events, all of history spirals upon itself. The One collapses the spiral into the dimension where it chooses to exist and there is no time nor space. All is at once. Life is a spiral of events unfolding existing without time and space. *As you awaken into your sovereignty you will see that it is nothing to collapse the spiral and enjoy the view at your leisure.*

Why then does all the human frailty come up? Why was I so bulimic just the night before, while editing my website pieces with apparent clarity. *You must be more gentle with yourself. It's silly really and lucky that you have a good sense of humor. All the issues of ego and self-delusion are like scum at the bottom of the pond which get swirled up to the surface of the heart chakra to be blown away by the winds of change. All the birthing anxiety you feel before the process is the human effort to maintain balance in the roiling waters.*

I asked about my vision of reflection in the bowl of water that is my heart chakra. Must I be still in order to allow others to see themselves? Yes and no. Won't the waters become stagnant if not flowing? *The waters are living, flowing in and out of the heart chakra. According to the level of awakening of the being is the depth of clarity. What appears to be still is moving and alive, an organic, interactive process.*

182

I asked about sovereignty, the levels of awakening. *You are imagining awakening as a hierarchy with steps or levels like a ladder. That is the third dimensional view, part of the old paradigm. The fourth dimensional view is one of deepening. The deeper you become, the closer to the One. The depths exist within the bowl you call the heart chakra.* I just wanted to dive in! It was like some of my dolphin dreams when I dive in deeply and can breathe, swimming with absolute freedom.

The grand finale unveiled the truth that I have always known. I was delighted.

Thinking about my corporate advisor's bugging me about a strategic plan, I asked, "Did You have a strategic plan?"

The One laughed, "Of course, it's in the DNA. The DNA is the strategic plan for all life." I guess you have to ground it into reality for it to manifest. Even the One continues to change through the evolutionary process.

Of course it is the DNA. I have always known it. I have expressed it in my countless works, lectures, interactions, dreams. Yet this is much more simple. We all need a strategic plan to base our life upon to refer to in times of trouble, so that the flow is directed, understood. The strategic plan is encoded in our DNA. All creatures have DNA, all are part of life. We have never been abandoned on this earth plane. We were given a perpetual strategic plan for existence, for enlightenment. It has been within all the while.

Part Seven
REFLECTIONS ON THE PATH

51. CHAKRAS AND MEDITATION

My oldest friend is at it again. Who knew that our reconnection would be such a source of inspiration for me? The universe perhaps? Our souls? Well, she asked to borrow any books I had on chakras and meditation. She couldn't find anything online. I said sure. I'll look through my library and see what I've got. So I went through my spiritual library. I've kept every book that has touched my soul but alas, I found nothing. How did I learn about chakras and such if not from books?

That got me thinking. When I first heard about chakras...I think it was about the time I met my first mentor...I felt I already "knew" these power points. They were in perfect alignment with the endocrine system — the glands that produce hormones. The words used to describe the energy of the chakras — which by the way means wheels of energy in Sanskrit — were exactly how I would describe the hormonal effects from each gland. I see the same colors from root to crown when I assess a patient. The only difference I have with the traditional Eastern interpretation of these power points lies in the second chakra.

So in my interpretation of how East meets West in the endocrine system, the first chakra corresponds with the gonads. Known as the root chakra, the first chakra is red, the color of passionate creation, the fire of creation. The ovaries of a woman and the testes of a man produce the hormones necessary to "create" new life and rebirth themselves. When people enter the midlife crisis, it is truly a time of recreating their new life. Helping them with bio-identical hormone replacement therapy has been my biological therapies, while I help them understand that in order to get that clear deep red passion back in their lives, they must conceive a new passion. Usually this leads to a new life via art, hobbies, change in occupation, finally finding their soul purpose. Those patients with issues of the first chakra—prostate cancer, ovarian cysts, uterine fibroids—I find to be stuck in their creativity. While we may conceive an idea in our brains, it is through this red root chakra that we birth our creations. I "see" the first chakra as taking root into the earth where we birth our creative powers of manifestation.

The second chakra corresponds to the pancreas. Known as the belly or umbilical chakra, the second chakra is bright orange, very sweet, the fuel to the fire of creation. Like insulin escorting glucose into your cells to create energy, the second chakra is your source of creative energy, fueling or nurturing your creations. I call this the sweetness of life. I see very few people with bright orange second chakras. Most of what is diagnosed as insulin resistance is at the spiritual level a resistance to the sweetness of life. Once a patient opens to receive the sweetness of life, her blood sugar stabilizes, she no longer needs to store body fat around her middle like a buoy, her insulin resistance reverses. Not that I do not recommend supplementation to biochemically treat insulin resistance but without the energetic connection, the healing is incomplete.

The third chakra corresponds to the adrenal glands. The adrenals sit atop of your kidneys and are the energetic source of power. They produce the stress hormones of fight or flight. This chakra located at the level of your solar plexus is bright yellow — a place of energetic balance of will and emotion. I find that fear related disease sits here. Don't you feel fear in the pit of your stomach? Well, that is your third chakra. This is the chakra most of the first world power hungry population is working on. This is the chakra where my bulimia resided…the pit of fear. Although I rarely meet a truly yellow aura, I've come to love this golden energy however briefly encountered. It feels like delight.

Warm, bright sunshiny, long summer days filled with joy. That is a healthy third chakra.

The fourth chakra corresponds with the thymus. Known as the heart chakra, the fourth chakra is all about learning to love self and others. It is green with a rosy center. The heart chakra is expansive. I've had experiences of my heart chakra feeling as large as the ocean…deep and green with all the colors merged within it…where I am connected to all that is…through my heart. The thymus is a tiny gland that programs your white blood cells to know the difference between self and other to protect you. This is where we form healthy boundaries. Heart centered compassion begins with self-love. I've heard that Buddhist monks must learn compassion for self before committing themselves to compassionate service to others. This is a hard lesson for we've been acculturated to accept martyrdom and self-sacrifice as the means to salvation. Yet if you do not care for yourself, how can you care for others? It's like the safety instructions given on the airplane. Put your own oxygen mask on first then help those dependent upon you. Makes sense, doesn't it?

The fifth chakra corresponds with the thyroid. Known as the throat chakra, the fifth chakra is blue, clear and bright as a summer sky. The thyroid controls metabolism, how fast we burn energy. The fifth chakra orchestrates how we express ourselves, how we use energy. Do we speak our truth? If not, dis-ease sets in, usually as thyroid disorders, chronic sore throats, laryngitis. All her life, my mother was not able to wear necklaces…she felt as if she was choking to put anything around her throat. A classic fifth chakra issue. Through my own spiritual journey, I have worked through my chakras and just before my 50th birthday felt like I needed topaz to fully open my fifth chakra. My mother found a beautiful silver choker embedded with blue topaz in the form of a butterfly. Perfect gift for my transformation. Perfect timing to finally speak my truth by telling my story.

The sixth chakra corresponds with the pituitary gland. Known as the third eye, the sixth chakra is indigo (notice how the colors of the chakras are in rainbow alignment). The seat of insight, inner knowing, consciousness, the sixth chakra houses the pituitary which regulates the lower endocrine system. Although most refer to the pituitary as the master gland, I like to think of it as a middle manager, since it responds to hypothalamic hormones. The true Queen of the kingdom, the hypothalamus controls the entire neuro-immune-endocrine system. But that's another topic fully illustrated in my best-selling book- Hormones in Harmony®.

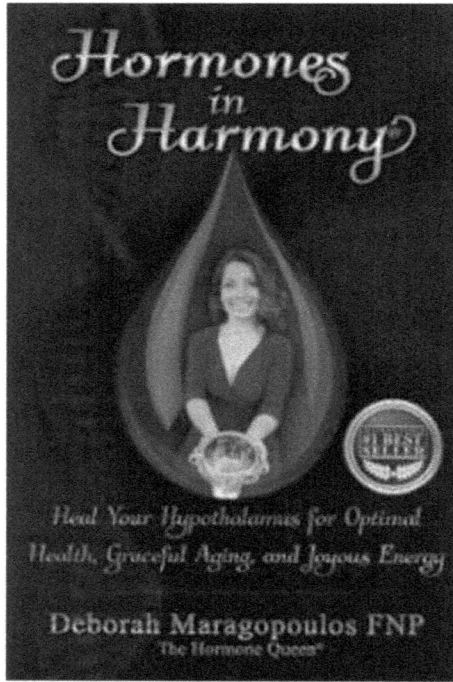

The seventh chakra corresponds with the pineal gland. Known as the crown chakra, the seventh is violet. I always imagine bowing my head in prayer and receiving divine enlightenment through my crown—white light refracting into the rainbow. When the sun goes down, the pineal gland produces the sleep hormone melatonin and our subconscious communicates with

190

us through dreams. The crown chakra tends to be very open in what I call ethereal people while their lower chakras especially their roots are closed. They appear to me as bubbleheads with their aura concentrated around their head. It seems to me that each of us has a dominant color to our life force. A violet life force often directs a person towards serving humanity through the healing arts, although I imagine this life force would make a good sage, priestess, wise man. I've been told by energy healers that I have a violet aura. I do see violet whenever I meditate and violet is a power color for me.

An indigo life force is unusual in adults. You might have heard of the Indigo Children. It is believed that these children of the new age are born with clear insight, deep inner knowing, and many gifts including clairvoyance, clairaudience and clairsentience. There's a lot of speculation of when these children began to arrive, but the majority seemed to be born around the Harmonic Convergence from the early 80's to the mid 90's. An indigo life force would seem to guide one into world changing professions and fields. My son is indigo, not an easy aura to have as he grew up, yet is coming into resonance the closer we get to the shift.

A blue life force serves an orator, teacher, politician very well. A green life force seems to direct people into the service fields, agriculture, and environmental sciences. These seem to be salt of the earth, grounded balanced people. My husband has a green life force. Most people I have met with yellow auras seem to be very fearful, tend to have lots of anxiety. I believe that a healthy yellow life force would guide one into many fields of service as you would be empowered by love rather than fear reactive.

Orange auras are rare indeed. I think an orange life force would make amazing parents, especially mothers, but anyone who nurtures new young life would find great ease if they possessed an orange life force. People with red life forces build our world — artists, contractors, technologists, scientists, producers. Red empowers their creative forces and they live life passionately, although may not be easy to live with being fueled by a great survival instinct.

Whatever your dominant life force, all your chakras need to be in balance to stay healthy. I love to do a chakra meditation in which I am climbing a mountain of color. I lie or sit with my hands in a V, fingertips down between my legs to focus my energy in my root and begin my journey into self. I begin at the base of the mountain where the path is red. All the flowers and trees and rocks and even the path itself are shades of red. Often I am met by a red escort, sometimes male, sometimes female, always very sensual, passionate, hot energy. As I ascend the mountain, I can feel my energy rising from my root chakra into my belly. And the path shifts to reddish orange until it is bright and juicy as a naval orange.

Surrounded by orange foliage accompanied by an orange guide whose energy is very sweet, tender, I rise up my mountain of energy. The colors shift into mango, sunset orange-yellow. When I enter a bright yellow part of the path with golden sunflowers and wheat colored grasses, I feel a lightness in my solar plexus, like all my worries have been drained from me. A golden escort brings me higher up the mountain until I meet the green man. Here my escort is always male, perhaps because I see him as the divine masculine part of myself. I feel filled with love, an expansiveness in my chest that extends into my arms through my entire body and out beyond my aura. If I stay here long enough I feel a connection with all that is like I am an ocean of potential. The green path is very natural, earthy, very familiar and I can stay here forever, but the green man always encourages me to go on to the blue part of the journey. The colors shift from green to turquoise to sky blue. All the flowers, the trees, the grasses are a strange but peaceful shade of blue.

Here any constriction in my throat relaxes and often I feel like singing. Although the song is wordless, it feels like the sound of my chakras—OH, AHH, OO, EE—a blessed relief. Here I may meet a blue escort, but more likely it is the wind blowing me through this part of my journey. The blue deepens, darkens until it is indigo in color and I feel perched within my own head, as if I am looking in behind my eyes. The mountain path is narrow and shorter now, intensely indigo blue. Like the deepest dye of blue jeans, it stains my perception, everything looks indigo. I am nearly there and stay on this part of the path very briefly.

At the top of the mountain I ascend white marble steps into a crystalline temple. Any garments I may be wearing fall away as I enter a clear pool of water. All my energy fields are cleansed as the water bathes away my fears, doubts, worries, disbelief. I step out of the pool and into a violet flame. Any negativity I have carried into the temple of my being is transformed by this flame into a gemstone. Sometimes the gem is yellow topaz if my work has been centered in clearing fear from my third chakra. Sometimes it is sapphire blue if my focus has been on speaking my truth. The transformation of my negative energy into a gem is a transmutation of poisons into gifts. I leave the gem as a gift to my temple. My crown chakra at this point feels very wide open, yet I am quite grounded. My lower chakras well lit, experienced and cherished keep me in my form, in the temple of my body. Once I set down my gift, I get to enjoy the view. The temple sits upon the mountain of my life and from here I can see where I've been and where I'm going, in fact all of my potentials lie before me, paths untaken, paths yet to explore. It is quite wondrous. Sometimes I am in need of guidance and if so I am met by a guide, an angel, more often than not an embodiment of my Higher Self. We sit in conference or stroll the temple gardens and I receive insight.

Sometimes I am taken to an inner room where my ancestral memory resides. Some refer to this as the Akashic records. I don't spend much energy there, receiving the connections from the past, from my DNA, from my soul agreements and bridging them to my present existence. Sometimes I am in need of healing so I am taken to a healing room where I lie or rather levitate while I am being ministered to by what feels like angels. When I am through with my meditation, I slide or slip or dance back down the path to the point where my fingertips meet at my root.

52. SEVEN LAYERS OF SOUL LESSONS

Our chakras provide a guide to our life lessons. Layers discovered as we dive deeper into our selves. I wrote this piece a few years ago and left it for my son to review. Being an old soul and one endowed with deep compassion, his insights are invaluable. He left a copy in the bathroom where my brother-in-law discovered it. I was surprised by what my husband's brother, not a well read or educated man, had to say.

"Deb, I read those soul layers you wrote about. It's true! I'm definitely dealing with my yellow layer! But at least there's hope!"

I gave him a hug and thanked him for his insight. Truth is truth. If you're open to receive the gift of each encounter, then you recognize what is true for you.

♥   Red Layer: represents first chakra. It's all about survival. We struggle to make our way through tough life lessons. Most of humanity barely survives life's lessons. Not yet searching for meaning, those of us who do make it celebrate our survival from dis-ease, loss, trauma, etc. It's as if we fought a war and won. We honor survivors. If they can do it, then so can we.

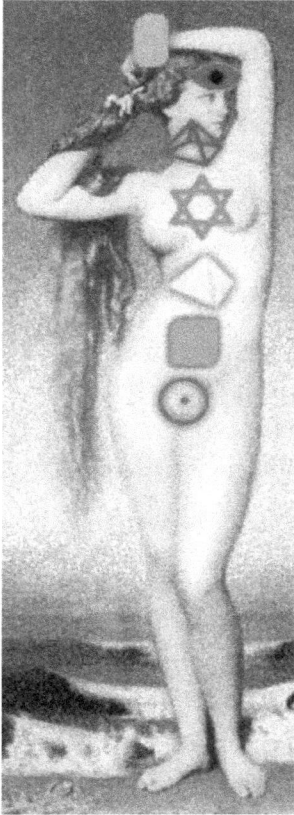

♥ Orange Layer: represents second chakra. It's all about gathering the sweetness of the lesson and trying to move on. We look for meaning in the lesson — what we learned. We love the "enlightened sayings" of those who appreciate the sweetness of life. It makes us feel good to share our hard-earned wisdom, to read about or watch others' stories that seem to end happily. It gives us hope. Receiving the blessing of the lesson is where forgiveness begins.

♥ Yellow Layer: represents third chakra. It's all about balancing will and emotion. Although this is a deeper layer, it feels less than. You thought you learned your lesson and here it is like a bad rerun rearing its ugly head. You know you should feel better about the lesson, but fear creeps in as it repeats itself again and you try to will it away, move on, not stoop to just surviving as you did in the beginning. You try to count your blessings but the sweetness has become bitter. Time to release your fear. This is the place most of us get stuck. This is what wears us out, makes our adrenals crash, our health fail, we wish to die.

♥ Green Layer: represents the fourth chakra. It's all about compassion…for self! Here we learn to love ourselves. There is an energy of gratitude for our humanness. This is the deepest level of forgiveness when we can be grateful for the players in the drama of our lives. Those who seem most enlightened exist here. They express compassion to others for they have learned self-compassion. The beloved teachers and gurus have shown us how to be human and live in the heart. But more lessons are to come…

♥ Blue Layer: represents the fifth chakra. It's all about truth. Your truth. Fully digesting the lesson and expressing the divine truth of the lesson in your life's work. You have grown tremendously from the first time you faced this lesson. When it repeats itself, you are able to graciously receive it and name its truth. Being embodied on earth gifts us with soul baring opportunities to know our selves intimately. This is when the teachers are quoted and become immortalized.

♥ Indigo Layer: represents the sixth chakra. It's all about insight. You now have deep insight into the lesson as you relive it a sixth time. Quickly you survive, receive the sweetness, release the fear, feel compassion for yourself, express the truth of the lesson and become the gnosis.... the experiential divine. You need not speak your truth to BE your truth. You exist in harmony with all life, following spirit deeply into this lesson without struggle. Yet one more time you will revisit the lesson in this life or another or perhaps beyond the human existence...one more time...

♥ Violet Layer: represents the seventh chakra. It's all about multidimensional connection. This is where Heaven meets Earth in you. You now have the Divine perspective. You understand the purpose of your humanity. You appreciate your emotions as vehicles to higher, deeper manifestations of Love. You are truly enlightened in regards to this lesson. Finally you are free…

Time for another sacred lesson ☺

53. GRATITUDE HEALS

I've been going through my journals looking for clues to how I got to where I am. I have journals dating back to 1975. I've kept everything I have ever written in my mother's old cedar chest. Her hope chest carries my past.

In October 2007, I was just about to launch <u>LoveDance</u>® into the world and was in a place of profound appreciation …

I am in deep gratitude for the blessings in my life, for:

- Steve—for his passion, protection, partnership
- Jarys—for teaching me compassion and courage
- Kyra—for embodying love and delight

- Mom — for buoying my spirit
- Dad — for seeding my existence
- Sisters — for opening to possibility
- Friends — for supporting my dreams
- Patients — for believing in me
- Colleagues — for challenging my mind
- Enemies — for challenging my heart
- Home — for sheltering my soul
- Community — for encompassing my passion
- Nation — for the freedom to expand
- Planet — for sustenance to be
- Divine Mother — for my glorious form
- Divine Father — for my expansive soul
- Divine Son — for my creative mind
- Divine Daughter — for my passionate heart

I still feel the same, thank the Divine. It's good to count your blessings. It's better than keeping count of your woes. Much more healing. Besides. Gratitude opens up your heart to love. A good place to start.

At the grandmother's council, I learned about an ancient Hawaiian forgiveness prayer. Whenever there is a disagreement among the people, the elders hold the offending parties in a circle of energy until each can truthfully say to the other:

I'm sorry

Please forgive me

Thank you

I love you

What a great example of how gratitude morphs into love. I believe the prayer means:

I'm sorry — I recognize my part in orchestrating such drama to learn my soul lessons.

Please forgive me — I ask forgiveness of all those in the wake of my human drama and I forgive myself.

Thank you — I am in deep gratitude for your humanity.

I love you — In loving your divine self, I am able to love my divine self.

Next time you are feeling angry and frustrated with someone else, do this meditation. Sit quietly with your hands resting in your lap. Take a deep breath and with the exhalation release everything that doesn't serve you. Repeat the breath two more times breathing deeper and deeper until it feels as if you are breathing all the way to your fingertips where they meet at your root. Now imagine the other person as a bubble of energy. I like to imagine their life color, but you can picture their face if you wish. Then say each line of the Hawaiian forgiveness prayer out loud really trying to feel the energy of each line:

I'm sorry
Please forgive me
Thank you
I love you

Repeat as many times necessary to feel love and gratitude for the other person and for yourself.

54. SHIFTS IN CONSCIOUSNESS

These are the eight shifts of consciousness humans make to enlightenment. I heard them listed as such in a recorded channeling... (that's the first shift...is it real?) ...yet always knew this order for I have been living it. Yet it's nice to see it outlined. The order is not absolute...the process is more like fading or dying...a slow shift of color...bleeding into one another as the phases of the shifts blend...the first two are in order...the rest seem to me to get stronger, more prevalent, more absolute in your life over time... I think this is a nice way to organize My Story. I wonder if it will fit neatly into eight sections...probably not, for as soon as I try to organize my existence, I begin to flow into chaos...always creating... Well, here they are...The 8 Shifts of Consciousness:

1.   **Curiosity** — You ask what's real? This is the beginning. You're awakening! Yeah!

I think I skipped this stage since it's always seemed real to me. I really didn't realize that what was real for me didn't seem real to others until I was a teenager. Then I began to play the human game and that included disconnecting myself through my eating disorder. Then I fell in love. And love reconnected me to my truth. It was all real to me.

2.   **Belief** — You know it's real and you want to know more. You search for answers. You seek gurus. You read books. You go to seminars. You still have a human approach of limited 3D

perception and conditioned judgment. And you wonder if anyone else feels the same. When you receive proof, you want others to share in your enlightenment. You may be a little evangelistic.

This was my guru stage. My family thought I was joining cults...so different had I become. I began to find their energy difficult to be with...yet my new friends came and went in my life, attracted to my light as I was attracted to theirs, but you don't shine very bright in a room full of light, so you seek dark places to illuminate. Through karma and drama, they slipped out of my life and I learned to be the light in any situation.

3.   **Light & Dark** – You make sense of light and dark, understanding over time that both exist in you. And in each one of us. And eventually you get to experience how darkness is just the absence of light and you begin to understand that fear is the absence of love. Then you begin to love yourself. Fill yourself with light and your fear, your darkness becomes illuminated.

I really got this finally...after dreaming I was Mary Magdalen. Then I made sense of fear and darkness. Really before I could not see the darkness in others, only the light. I knew my darkness and judged it harshly. Shining my light brightly outside of self, so that my shadow loomed bigger and bigger behind me. Shatan, get behind me!

4. **Karma** — You get off the karmic wheel! Yeah! You eliminate karmic imprints and no longer live under predestined energy. Now your future is yours to create.

I worked on this a long time...well before I knew what karma meant. I was born feeling a sense of predestination...of having a mission to complete, but also very much aware that I was creating my reality...a strange paradox and difficult to do before 1987. In 1987, I made a great shift...I learned much later that was the time of the Harmonic Convergence...it seems as I am always on time for all the major shifts in consciousness, feeling the energy and dancing with the flow without a need to know. My need to make sense of all this came later...when I met the gurus and they had names for what I had always felt. It's as if I never really went to sleep but stayed conscious all my life, knowing that my time would come. And it has. The karmic imprint retreat was the last of entanglements. These stages overlap. It took a long time, nearly to ascension to clear the last karmic imprint.

5. **Illumination** — You send light to the rest of the planet. This takes practice not to send your bias and judgment along

with your light. You focus the light of peace into a war raged zone…yet it is not your light, but divine light…and those warring parties may need to wake up and become a bit more conscious before they can live in peace. So you send light…divine light from your heart-soul to theirs and they will receive the illumination necessary to make their own shifts. Here is where you begin to change matter, to affect the elements, to consciously create your reality.

Being a healer helped me learn this concept of not biasing my light. In the beginning, of course I felt frustrated when my patients would not follow my enlightened recommendations for their health and wellbeing, but I learned that I was not healing them but that they were coming for illumination, to receive my healing light of potential and then they would use that light or not…it was their choice. I always felt uncomfortable praying for others, sending group energy to others imbibed with our wishes for them. How did we know what's best for them at the soul level? So I send light and love. I've been signing all my correspondence with this intimacy for many years. I send you light and love…you may do with it what you will…it is not for me to put conditions on my love or my light…

6. **Synchronicity** — You begin to recognize synchronicity. You realize that these amazing events that lead to your shift in consciousness are not coincidence but synchronistic. You begin to live in an interdimensional way…not that you are not already interdimensional…there are aspects of you in all the dimensions…past, present, and future…but you know it now and realize that you are one of many human chess pieces on the grand board of life on earth and that you are controlling the game…your god-self, your higher self, in synchronicity with their god-selves, their higher selves.

I've always loved synchronicity. It's hard to remember a time when I didn't recognize the synchronicity in my life. I knew everything that happened was not against me but for me…I have always received the gifts of life, transmuting what seems like poisons to others into illumination for myself and my loved ones. Receiving the synchronistic events like presents…I am grateful for each and every one. The sooner I learned to express my gratitude and receive the fullness of the gift of synchronicity, the faster I moved along my path of enlightenment.

7. **Self-Healing** — You can heal yourself! Whether you understand the "technology" of upregulating your DNA or not,

you know that you can heal yourself through intention…and you do.

Again, I used my will to affect my life, including healing myself…yet didn't understand what I was doing until I had an accident on my horse in 2002. About the same time I let go of all my gurus…meaning I no longer looked to them to heal me (healers either do not allow anyone else to help them, or they are always looking outside of self for healing). I was gifted by an opportunity to heal myself. I knew at a mental, intellectual, scientific level how to up-regulate my DNA…yet had not the "gnosis" — the experience of healing myself at the genetic level. And with all my knowledge, my healing came down to being my body's best cheerleader and I healed myself miraculously and quickly.

Now it seems that there is not a "one-time" healing for all time, but you will get opportunities to practice and refine your skills. You don't need a major dis-ease like cancer to do this…I have been warding off contagious dis-ease with a little mantra. I place my hands in a V at my root chakra and say "This is not my bug!" It always works. Just that little conscious instruction to my immune system. As for aging, I have placed all my intentions into my Genesis Gold® and believe it is giving me everything I need to manifest health and wellbeing for my second 50 years on earth...or perhaps longer, I'll decide then ☺ Because I have intended healing at the genetic level into my creation, Genesis Gold® helps others who also believe in the possibility that they can turn on healing genes. They don't need to know how for it to work. My mother asked if I had casted a magic shield around her...for she saw so many women her age and they're old! I told her that she had allowed Genesis Gold® to affect not just her physicality but her attitude. In truth, she's always had this power... I am spending a lot of time on this subject because it is what I try to help my patients tap into—their divine ability to heal themselves.

So why do those who profess enlightenment continue to challenge themselves with poor health? This is a good question and one that continued to plague me with my judgment of others for such a long time. I know now that we each experience our divinity in our own unique ways, that my way is not their way and vice versa. There is no ONE way! And that includes self-healing. This is a hard lesson...most healers are great at healing others but not themselves. And the enlightened ones I met with such physical challenges made me wonder how enlightened they really were...but now I see that self-healing is a late stage on the path...self-healing leads to ascension...for then you are an embodiment of full genetic potential, all 12 layers!

8.   **Ascension**—You finally arrived! Congratulations. But wait. You haven't gone anywhere. You're still right here on earth. How can that be? Doesn't Ascension mean you ascend to heaven? Well, heaven is here on earth. If you are ascended, you know that there is only here…and interdimensional aspects of this moment you might play in anytime you wish. The past and future and here and there are yours! You are not the same person you used to be.

I always knew I would not be the same after 50 and I am not. My friend saw the difference in me. I feel different. I feel as if my life is renewed. There is a great peace dancing in the flow of life. Seems strange at first…very different than my old way of being. Not that I've cast off all my humanity…No way! I still have passionate emotion. And I know fear…and darkness…and I see it in others, finally…yet I am living consciously, choosing love over fear, being the light that I am and knowing that all who come to me are attracted to the light and that is my true mission to reflect their own divine light back to them. And what's being asked of me at the divine level of consciousness is that I be a Master. I seem to be affecting others just by showing up…it's been going on for a long time…yet now I go with the flow and am gracious with my humanity when I am struggling a bit in the river of consciousness. I knew a Master once. He exuded light and love to all. They ended up worshipping Him. Yet I knew another side of Him…a very human side…the one who struggled with what he believed to be his mission…yet that is another story…

No one's perfect, not even Him…which is really great for the rest of us…that this body is the vehicle for our enlightenment and that our lives and especially our relationships are the path of our enlightenment. And that is why I am telling My Story.

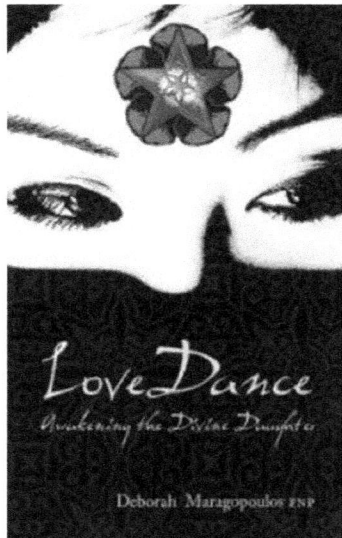

I told Hers in <u>LoveDance®: Awakening the Divine Daughter.</u>
Now it's time for the modern version....

55. TO HEAL SELF

A heavily laden fog dripped down my mare's legs as she pranced excitedly beneath me one damp Friday morning in late September. Holding the slick reins in check, I hesitated at the crest of the trail. As the steep wet asphalt lay disturbingly before us, a premonition caught my breath. I saw my mare fall trapping me underneath her. Well aware that thought creates reality, I tried to clear my mind and rode on.

Not fifty yards later, my mare spooked and in an effort to stop her from bolting, I turned her up the sharp grade. She slipped and, as if rehearsed, I vaulted off her back. Thankfully not pinned under a thousand pounds of terrified horse, I managed to save my skull from what would have been a concussive blow, landing instead...on my mouth. Scrambling to my feet, I ran after her, touching my bloodied lip to extract my front teeth.

Thanks to a kind gardener/caballero, I caught my runaway horse and made it home first tending to her wounds, my teeth in my pocket. Typical of most healers, I am reluctant to ask for help, but my husband perceived my unspoken distress and jumped out of bed having worked the graveyard shift to drive me to the emergency dentist.

The dentist shook his head when I handed him the cup of milk in which my broken teeth floated. "I cannot replace these…"

Patting his arm, I encouraged him, "I know you can do it. Please, you must believe in your ability."

While I prayed, focusing on the living essence of my teeth with healing intentions, he performed the procedure, then made me promise to go to the emergency room for x-rays. Although I did everything the dentist recommended as well as all the holistic remedies I would have prescribed for someone with similar injuries, I bemoaned my ill fortune.

My face was a mess—my nose, lips and chin skinned, swollen and bruised—like I had been beaten. I called my sister, who cried, "Oh, Deb, your beautiful teeth!" No braces, no cavities, straight and strong, my vanity lied in the perfection of my teeth. How could this have happened? I taught my patients that everything happens for a reason, but I couldn't see why. I even called my spiritual mentor, who provided only practical advice. I was on my own.

I believe each of the seven chakras of the body deliver purposeful messages, so what was this fifth chakra, which represents speaking one's truth, saying? I fell asleep wondering and awoke Saturday at dawn to meditate in nature.

Surrounded by my animals, even my very sore but sorry mare, I sat at the edge of a huge ugly gaping hole. We had just moved into the country and having lived through one unbearably hot summer began construction on a swimming pool. Our land was scarred and so was I. My mare nuzzled my back, while the dogs whined piteously with me.

Suddenly, I heard a voice. Not that small quiet voice that compassionately guides but one so obnoxious that the animals gave me a wide berth.

Stop feeling sorry for yourself. You've been given a gift...practice what you preach and heal yourself.

I actually smiled, cracking my scabbed lips, but I didn't care. This accident was a gift! Hugging my horse, I thanked her. Have you ever seen a horse smile? Remember Mr. Ed showing his big teeth, well, that's what she did, smiled at my recognition of her part on my soul's path.

Then I hurried in the house and took a good look in the mirror. Instead of seeing a broken reflection, I saw the healing. I became my own best cheerleader. I told my body what a great job it was doing every time I washed my wounds. I blessed every herbal supplement for helping my system recover. Every ounce I drank in gratitude (dentist's orders — no solid foods) praying that each nutrient find its way to repair the damage.

And by Monday, I was whole and healed, not a single scar. A couple of days later, I went back to the emergency room to pick up some x-rays and the nurses didn't recognize me. Oh, yes, and to the dentist's great surprise, my teeth took root.

Healing is an innate power within each and every one of us. It is encoded, I believe, in the unexpressed DNA, ready to be turned on by the power of our intentions. The National Cancer Institute has reported success in treating melanoma patients by genetically altering their white blood cells to enhance the ability of the immune system to kill cancer. In early cancer research, success means any cure since researchers tend to get medical failures to experiment on, so perhaps the 13 out of 15 subjects who were not cured had their immune systems destroyed by radiation and chemotherapy. The power to heal via a strong and vibrant immune system is innate.

I believe that clear intention and pure desire can turn that unexpressed DNA on, so perhaps the two melanoma patients who were cured believed so valiantly in the therapy that their hopes and prayers enabled their disabled genetics to remember how to fight off cancer.

As a healer, I have learned that I do not heal anyone, but educate them to heal themselves. I provide biochemical and psycho-spiritual counsel. I hold the intention, the energy of health and well-being mirrored in my body, in my DNA. Once a young woman I had been seeing since her teens insisted on an office exam just six months after her annual pap smear. There was no medical reason for her to come, so I questioned her. She very eloquently answered, "I just need to sit in your presence, feel your vibration, and I am set for about half year."

I have a dear older patient, who makes me promise after every visit, every phone call to stay well. "We need your vibrancy to remember how to be whole."

After working all my life to be an example of health through exercise, nutrition, and lifestyle choices, I know that my true talent is in perceiving every event in my life as a lesson. Plus a positive attitude can be seriously protective.

Once in Seattle, I attended a detoxification seminar. After the morning presentations about all the toxins in our everyday environment, we were released for lunch. This group of holistic nurses, physicians, naturopaths and chiropractors hesitated to choose anything from the menu of what seemed to be a reasonably healthy restaurant. With my usual gusto, I ordered tuna on fire and the rest of them looked at me like I was nuts. One woman asked if I had paid attention to the statistics on heavy metal contamination of fatty fish.

"Why, yes. I took scrupulous notes, but I do not believe in my vulnerability to toxicity. At this very moment, your fear is sucking the mercury right out of my tuna." True, although I have eaten contaminated seafood all my life, I have not tested positive for heavy metal toxicity. Was it favorable genetics, perhaps...or my attitude?

Whenever I see a seriously contagious patient, I say to myself, "This is not your bug!" and rarely catch their illness. When I do become ill, it is usually a psycho-spiritual dilemma in which I have been paying little attention and finally my body is reminding me to take care of it.

My accident was truly a gift. I had never been seriously injured before in spite of vigorous and dangerous activities — mountain biking, skiing, scuba diving, road bike racing — never given a personal chance to learn how healing works.

What I learned was this: that gratitude is the key to the power of intention. With all the positive encouragement, my body rapidly responded. It makes me wonder how much faster I might have healed if I didn't spend the first day fussing over my predicament. Fear definitely hampers healing. Surely I have seen this to be true.

Years ago, I had diagnosed a 32-year-old patient with metastatic breast cancer. Granted, I was well trained in western medicine and was dabbling in natural therapies, but cancer? She was not just a patient, but a co-worker, a friend, my age and very much concerned about her husband's fifteen-year-old niece, who was fretting over her young healthy breasts, fearful of developing her aunt's cancer. I taught the girl how to examine herself, explained that she shared none of her aunt's risk factors, they weren't even related, but shortly after we buried her aunt, the girl developed a tumor. In the exact same spot.

Mind over matter? I was taught then and there the power of thought when fueled by fear. And I have seen over and over again, patients worrying themselves into disease...yet I have also seen the power of hope, love and gratitude to cure what was deemed incurable.

Bernie Segal, the author of <u>Love, Laughter, and Medicine</u>, was one of the first allopathic doctors to explore the curative power of love. He stated case after case of illnesses derived by suggestion — like the man who was just about to be discharged from the hospital but told instead by an intern that he had only days to live and died — as well as the cures — like the man whose family decided not to tell him that his cancer was fatal and lived well beyond his physician's dire prognosis.

In my experience, most of my breast cancer patients tend to take care of everyone but themselves. Unless they receive that lesson, they do not survive the disease. I have some amazing women in my practice who have healed themselves by understanding that their cancer was their souls' cry for help, not attending to the souls' needs for so long that their body had to get their attention. Some use traditional allopathic treatments, others use only natural therapies, most who seek my care combine the two. I do not dictate to them what they must do to heal, what therapeutics to choose, but counsel them to make peace with their bodies, find the gift in their disease and begin healing with the faith that they have the innate ability to cure themselves.

Many of my patients come to me "hormonally-challenged". I coined this term years ago to describe not just the aging process or stress-related deficiencies, but also the resistance to our own bio-chemical messengers. You might have heard of insulin resistance leading to obesity and diabetes, but you can have cellular receptor site resistance to any of your own hormones produced by your gonads, adrenals, thyroid, even your pituitary gland.

If I diagnose an insulin resistant patient early and put him on a low glycemic diet and supplements to enhance cellular receptivity, but do not help him explore the fact that he may unconsciously feel unworthy of the sweetness in life, he will require more and more therapeutic assistance and the most strictly abstinent diet just to keep his blood sugars under control.

If he receives the gift of his insulin resistance and begins healing his sense of unworthiness, his cells open to receive the glucose necessary to run his metabolism. He becomes metabolically more active, loses that midline fat as well as the risk factors that would have led to diabetes and heart disease, but more so, he takes delight in life.

The spring before my accident, I attended a Science and Consciousness conference in Albuquerque and realized how I had healed myself. Gregg Braden spoke on his newest book, The Isaiah Effect, which explained that prayer and healing worked through clear intention fueled by loving gratitude. So with my experience and armed with the equation for manifestation, I began teaching my patients. Sometimes the Isaiah effect worked, but not always, especially in dealing with relationship issues.

I am not the only soul in the universe, but am part of a great whole, so when my intentions would not become manifest as rapidly as I desired, my husband would remind me that it's not in Deborah-timing, but Divine-timing.

The next year while researching my first novel, LoveDance®, I discovered Neil Douglas Klotz. His work explained that the terms translated as good and evil from the Aramaic, tava and bisha, actually meant—ripe and unripe. So Divine-timing meant Ripe timing.

We have been taught that the formula for manifestation was clear intent plus pure emotion is what creates our reality. But the formula is not algebraic, it's trigonometric. Not duality but trinity. There is a third part—ripe timing.

$$X + Y + Z = \text{Manifestation}$$

Whereas:

$$X = \text{Intention}$$
$$Y = \text{Emotion}$$
$$Z = \text{Timing}$$

Your Intention + Your Emotion + Divine Timing = Your Reality

So now I counsel my patients to continue to hold clear intentions of healing their bodies, their minds, their relationships; fuel their intentions not with fear but with loving gratitude; and in ripe-timing, they will manifest. And the rewards will be sweet indeed.

Every day, I thank my body for her strength, her health, her vitality. Like taking my nutraceutical supplement—Genesis Gold®—and staying active, I see gratitude as a proactive means to support my wellbeing. I am trying very hard to practice what I preach, so neither my body nor my inner voice must scream to get my attentions. And thankfully now that guiding voice has become a gentle whisper.

Part Eight
INTEGRATION

56. DISENTANGLE YOUR CORDS OF ATTACHMENT

Driving back home on Southern California freeways crowded with tourists taking advantage of the last glorious summer weekend…an ache in my breast, a dark shadow where the sun once shone, an eclipse in my existence…I left my daughter, my sunshine, at San Diego State University.

How long I've prepared for this transition, how many soulful meditations, how many intimate conversations with so many other mothers who have gone through this phase of life. Yet in spite of all my work, during that last kiss goodbye, the cords that bound our hearts pulled so tight to nearly snap.

I released my firstborn into the world four years before, but my daughter filled up the space that he left behind, so much so that now there is a void in my heart, in my home, in my life.

Having counseled my patients, hundreds of them, through life's transitions, I should know better, I should take my own advice. Haven't I told them how within the web of life, we float upon the river of consciousness, connected by invisible threads from heart chakra to heart chakra? Attached to everyone, and entangled with all we love, all we hate, all with whom we struggle.

So as a mother of an empty nest, some would advise that I cut the cord for her wellbeing and mine. But that is an old paradigm teaching and an illusion for we can never cut ourselves off from creation. We are all on the web, connected together. There is only one of us here. We are all part of the One Consciousness, all cells of the One Being. Every cell in my body knows it is a part of me just like I am a part of the earth and the sun, the plants and the creatures. Research by neuro-biologist, Candace Pert PhD, has shown that even when cells, tissues, or whole organs are removed, that the cells "remember" where they came from responding more like the donor than the transplant recipient. And I am connected to my daughter, imprinted since her birth, no matter how distant she is from me.

I know this to be true, because I can feel her emotion, especially her fear...it has wakened me up in the middle of the night when

226

she has most needed me. I trust this connection even more so than my vision. It has served me as a mother and especially as a healer. I feel my patients' dis-ease in the mirror of my being, but I have learned over the years not to embody their imbalances. Although connected to each and every one, I have learned to disentangle from the drama of being a healer and this is what I teach to my patients.

Imagine your life color as an infinitely strong gossamer thread emerging from your heart chakra to the heart of every other living thing. Each aspect of creation has its own color, born on the rainbow of light; its own vibration, its own sound. Imagine someone you are struggling with—your spouse, your child, your parent, your boss, whoever. What is their color? Imagine their cord and your cord braided together with knots scattered here and there. These knots represent your struggles, your difficulties in the relationship, your entanglements with each other.

Most of the people I counsel—my patients, my family, my friends—complain about the dramatic struggle within their relationships, know that they must make a change, come to me for help…and I tell them to disentangle from that being they are struggling with. We do the visualization together. They see their color, they see the color of the other person, they see themselves tied up in knots, they feel this entanglement literally as an ache in their breast, but when I begin to have them identify the knots in their cords of attachment, while they can name the problems that the knots represent, they have no idea how to untangle themselves. In fact, most are afraid, most claim they cannot let go.

Upon the river of consciousness, we all float, but entangled with others we struggle for breath, trussed together heart to heart, only one can breathe at a time, while the other holds her breath and prays. Everyone in our lives is a mirror to our souls, each reflecting back what we most need to learn, the judgments we hold of our humanity. What we like in another is what we appreciate in ourselves, what we dislike is what we need to change or accept in us.

How can you see in the mirror if your nose is pressed to the glass? That is why my patients struggle with disentanglement because they cannot see clearly what the lesson is in the struggle with another.

So I help them identify the most recent knot and going back in time a few more knots. Oh, they can name the knots, but not the gifts. What gifts? What could possibly be good about these struggles? Why, I tell them, every struggle is a gift that must be unwrapped. To receive the gift, first you must recognize it as a gift. Not all gifts have lovely exteriors in fact the most precious may be very ugly.

My Nana used to wrap up her garbage. Living in the city, the more compact the trash, the more likely the trash man would take it away, except Nana used to wrap it so nicely that Poppop would find it left on the step. The trash man thought it was a gift, so lovely was the wrapping. You see, you can't always tell by the wrapping; life's gifts are rarely wrapped so nicely.

My husband struggled with letting our daughter grow up. Once when he overstepped his parental boundaries, she told him after raising him for eighteen years she was done! He cried, "but I don't know how to let you go." She turned him over to me, "Mom, remember those cords of attachment? Dad needs your help."

So I explained the concept and he amazed me by visualizing their life colors just as I do. He is forest-green, she — golden as sunshine. He could see how they were tied together in a lovely fishtail braid, and he could see the knots, especially how they struggled with her growing independence, but he couldn't see the gift in lifting her curfew and allowing her some freedom before she took off to college. He could only see the sleeplessness until she arrived home at night, the worry about her making safe decisions. I pointed out that unlike his good friend who had not loosened the reins on his daughter, my husband after weeks of suffering adapted slowly albeit surely, finally falling asleep well before she arrived home. When she is away at college, he will rest, but his poor friend will not.

My husband agreed, but still struggled with receiving the gift of the knot, claimed, "I don't want to let her go." Heartbreakingly honest. Fearing to let go, fearing that we may not be able to float on our own in the river of consciousness, not trusting that we are still connected, we struggle and tighten the knots.

I did this same exercise while writing my first book, LoveDance®. I wrote from the perspective of the heroine and like most novelists I used those in my life to base my characters. Envisioning how "Mary" would disentangle her cords of attachment to "Teoma", I realized I must disentangle from my husband. For three days, he refused to go to work, sick to his stomach. I didn't have a chance, while nursing him, to do the meditation let alone write it. Finally, he returned to work and I opened myself to receive the gift of the encounter with my laptop. While writing Mary's disentanglement from Teoma, I disentangled my violet life cord from my husband's vibrant green. The knots of our most recent struggles all the way back to those formed when our first child was born prematurely. The older knots were so well fermented I could sip the sweet wine of their gifts easily. The more recent knots—like our struggle with our changing roles as parents and the interference writing a book brought to our daily life—were more acrid in their newness, but I took the bitter cup and using the lubrication of love, found the gifts.

Mary and I floated free, breathing easily in the river of consciousness, while Teoma struggled to cling to the bank feeling very much abandoned. The moment I pushed "save", my husband called. He was having a horrible day and "felt abandoned." In spite of my reassurance, it took three weeks of repetitive visualizations before he relaxed and I no longer felt the painful ache of his sense of abandonment mirrored in my heart.

Now I did this same visualization with my firstborn, disentangling my violet from their indigo. My knots of expectation in their success in school were more difficult to unravel than the original knot between us representing their difficult birth. All the challenges of their prematurity and their numerous endocrine problems became one of my most profound gifts. My first child is why I do what I do, why I became an expert in clinical neuro-immune-endocrinology. The more recent knot representing my struggle with allowing them to be on their own, trusting that they would be safe and happy in a world without my constant maternal influence was a bit more difficult. The well-hidden gift turned out to be…accepting my transformation as a mother from nurturer-protector to confidante-advisor. In accepting them, I accepted myself. Twenty-four hours after I loosened the last knot between us, my wise child called me from college in San Francisco. "What are you doing down there, Mom? I feel lighter than ever!" I explained the disentanglement and they encouraged me to continue and "let go of us all, even yourself, and see, how enlightened you can be."

So I did. Each and every significant person in my life, I disentangled from, I felt more and more free and my relationships with each person changed, transformed by love into something finer. I even disentangled from all I believed myself to be—a mother, a wife, a daughter, a sister, a healer, a woman, even from Deborah—and discovered my truth, which is joy.

Since disentangling from our daughter while she was a sophomore in high school, now that the time had come to let her grow up and go away to college, I am handling it better than I did with my first. With them, my body reminded me of the pain of birthing…I suffered from a sciatic condition (just like when I gave birth) that lasted from the moment I helped them fill out their college applications to the day I drove them up to the University of San Francisco. Now with my daughter, the pain is a bittersweet heartache, not physically manifested. The kind of ache that actually feels good, like watching a sad movie and crying your heart out and knowing the joy of being human is to feel passionately.

In fact, my ethereal connection with my children has been so acutely enhanced since disentangling from them, that I realize the knots of my entanglements interfered with the clarity of my perceptions. Since letting my daughter grow up, I sleep soundly, only twice bolting out of bed, feeling her panic and calmly contacting her (via the telephone, since telepathy is difficult through the veil of fear) and all was well. I've taught her to trust the inner knowing and realize that through trial and error she will learn to ride the wave of our ethereal connection.

Actually, when it came time to escort our daughter to college, my husband did pretty well. He cried of course, and while at first resisting disentanglement, he admitted to having worked on it and yes, he felt lighter, less fearful, more willing to let her go and trust she will be well. And we both began to receive the gift of her leaving, becoming closer than ever, falling in love all over again—just the two of us.

So how might you release the illusion of your entanglements? Envision your life color, whatever comes to you is fine, then envision the color of the other person. Your red cord and her blue cord are braided nicely for the most part, but knotted in places. Like a precious necklace entangled into the thread of a silk sweater you do not want to break either, but carefully loosen the knots using the lubrication of love.

I live near the beach and off the coast, derricks pump oil from the floor of the Pacific Ocean. Often I come home with tar stuck to the soles of my feet. Only oil gets it off—like dissolving like. These knots in your cords of attachment seem like tar, but they are gifts of love and only the lubrication of love can dissolve the knots. If you look with eyes of love you can find the gift in each knot. It's not easy, but after two or three knots, the entangled cords start unraveling, setting you free to float in the river of consciousness. You do not need to share with the person you are releasing what you have done, but your relationship WILL change.

No matter how ugly the wrapping, there is always a gift of love waiting to be discovered. So just let go. Disentangling your cords of attachment will free you to be your truth — the most precious gift of all.

57. MINING YOUR DNA

I've been teaching my patients for years that thought becomes manifest in our DNA. Our self-talk directs our DNA to dance accordingly…as healing or dis-ease. And Russian scientists have now proven it!

Consciously directing our DNA is why I created Genesis Gold®…I alchemized into the formula (which came to me in dreams) my heartfelt intention to optimize our genetic potential by balancing hormones, neurotransmitters and cytokines (tiny immune messengers) so our biochemistry sings harmoniously to our DNA. With the help of Genesis Gold®, many have healed themselves.

Healing at the genetic level is through a symphony of biochemicals that carry messages to the DNA. Most of us are born with DNA encoded for survival. If our communication networks are functioning properly then the DNA gets the proper messages to adapt to any situation. Dis-ease is more of a maladaptation to the environmental exposures and disharmonious energies.

We now have scientific proof that water has memory and can be imprinted with whatever it is exposed to. Since our bodies are made up of at least 60% water then it holds true that we can imprint our cellular fluids with healing through positive thoughts, nourishing foods and joyous experiences. I've "known" this to be true since I became a healer… my healing energies are imprinted in Genesis Gold® and every day I take it, I send blessings to all those who are drinking it with me.

When the Japanese earthquake sent radiation spilling into the ocean, many of my patients called concerned. I told them that first, Genesis Gold® has enough sea vegetation in it to protect their thyroid from radiation uptake, and second, that by promoting harmonious communication, they would adapt to whatever comes.

Your DNA has the best blueprint for your adaptation to any situation.

Imagine mining your DNA for gold: Health. Wellbeing. Longevity. Vitality. Greater Mental Abilities. Emotional Intelligence. More Refined Senses. Increased Sensitivity. Sacred Attributes. Well, you can.

I mine my DNA by swimming Fibonacci patterns. Diving under the water I imagine diving into myself, into my cells, into my own genetic code.

With each figure eight I swim, my mind clears, I relax into myself, and soon insight bubbles to the surface. I like to swim but you can do it anyway you please. The figure eight motion whether swimming, walking, dancing is meditative in itself.

Anytime I have a healing concern, I dive into myself. Usually my body will communicate back to me what is needed to heal: a change in diet, more sleep, different activities, a change in scenery.

Going more deeply, past the afflicted body part, into the tissues, the cells, finally into the DNA itself, I find what is needed may be a shift in consciousness.

First we must be open to change before healing transformation can begin. That's really the hardest part—being open to receive healing.

When healing seems evasive, I often wonder how I'm blocking healing. Usually it's emotional. Unresolved grief, unexpressed anger, or deep fear manifests itself as dis-ease. It's the emotion that may be blocking healing, even our own healing intentions.

Once I had a patient come to me to lose weight. So I counseled her on changing her sleep patterns (she was a night owl which contributes to insulin resistance and obesity), changing her diet (which was SAD—the Standard American Diet—high in calories, low in nutrients), begin exercising (she was completely sedentary with a daytime desk job) and most importantly to learn to love herself enough to make the changes necessary to get healthy.

238

She struggled with her weight…never quite ready to make all the changes necessary to get healthy. Oh, she dieted and would lose some weight. She started exercising and again weight would come off. She learned to sleep at night which improved her insulin resistance. Yet she was coming for help, out of fear of dis-ease, not out of love for herself. While we made some progress, it didn't stick.

Then she started taking Genesis Gold® and began noticing all the ways she was sabotaging herself. She described becoming a more compassionate observer of herself. She decided finally it was time to change for good.

She took the plunge. And discovered a deeply ingrained belief that was sabotaging her weight loss. Over time with more counseling and more work on her part to learn to love and appreciate herself, this patient got down to healthy weight and has remained there since. And she does not have to be so strict with her diet or obsessive with her exercise. She can even miss some sleep and not miss a beat. With the change of attitude and help of Genesis Gold® to balance her hypothalamus, her hormones, and her metabolism, she is manifesting her best self.

It takes much courage to dive into yourself and discover what is needed for your highest wellbeing. No one else can do this for you. You can be guided with visual imagery, hypnotized, counseled ad nauseum, yet ultimately, you must commit to yourself and take the plunge.

I created Genesis Gold® to help us tap into our greatest potential. It's all in our DNA, everything needed to be healthy. We are already whole. We just got to dive deep to discover the treasure. Go on, now, take the plunge!

58. TRANSFORMING YOURSELF

I began My LoveDance® the year I turned 50, fully expecting great change by 2012.

In the past four years, I've experienced even more change. I'm not the only one. Many of my patients and family and friends experienced major transitions since 2012.

More change. More death. So many deaths.

I meditated on this once after providing grief counseling for a half a dozen patients in as many days. Many were young, unexpected deaths.

Why are so many souls transitioning at this time?

And I saw:

A bridge of light between the dead and their loved ones. And the earth being pulled through their connection into the next dimension.

By dimension, I mean higher vibration. Like Love is a higher vibration than fear.

We are transforming, all of us, even the earth.

It's been a time of turmoil. A roller coaster of events creating great change. Some desired. Some unexpected. Some dreaded, but all needed. The whole world is transforming. People around the world are asking for change, gathering, protesting, demonstrating. The time is ripe for transformation. Why?

Because we cannot evolve without change. We have been like caterpillars consuming everything in our need to grow. And then it seems everything stood still…there was little growth…as if we were in a cocoon of our own making…some have called it a recession and financially perhaps it is, but I call it a transformation. For under the stillness, great change is occurring. The caterpillar is transforming into a butterfly. Soon the first of the butterflies will emerge.

You will see it as hope. Sweet happenings across the globe, in your neighborhood, perhaps in your own backyard…giving you hope…Like the feeling of wonder you get when you watch a butterfly emerge from a cocoon…then try its fragile wings in first flight. Hope.

So many have been cleaning house…our physical abodes and our subconscious as well. Getting rid of all that doesn't serve us…it's hard, but we must make room for the new. And you can't receive if your arms and heart are full of old stuff.'

I have been encouraging my patients to literally clean out their closets. When they have felt stuck, reliving old issues over and over again, seemingly making no progress, I encourage them to see this stuckness as a sign. It's time to clean their dwelling place. Start with the physical. Yes, their homes.

We all have stuff in our closets. Old stuff that once served us but no longer fits, no longer useful. Stuff we don't need anymore. Stuff that's just taking up space. So if you haven't used it for at least two years, you probably won't. Give it away. Sell it if you must. But get it out of your closets, out of your cupboards, out of your home.

Lighten up and make room for the new.

Cleaning out our homes at the physical level will help us clean out ourselves. And this time I'm not talking about a liver cleanse. I'm talking about cleaning out our psycho-spiritual closets.

Those old beliefs in our consciousness. You know the ones:

- I'm not good enough.

- I don't deserve better.

- I'm alone.

- Good things do not happen to me.

- I'm worthless.

- No one loves me.

- How can they? I don't even love myself.

We all have these imprinted beliefs. Perhaps we've lived a life highlighting these beliefs. Perhaps we were imprinted with these negative beliefs in childhood. Perhaps we came into this life with these feelings.

Either way. These NOT GOOD ENOUGH beliefs lie deep in our consciousness and are often at the root of our real problems...Our health problems. Our financial problems. Our relationship problems. Our problems being happy and feeling love.

So let's clear our closets. Let's let go of that which no longer serves us.

No one really likes change. We get too comfortable where we are. Even if where we are is not in our best interest. So it takes the Divine to give us the boot! Right out of our comfort zone and into a new reality.

We suffer because we don't know how to transform our selves gracefully.

I challenge each and every one of you to write down on a piece of paper everything in your closet that does not serve you. Everything... What are you ready to release?

- Your fear? Write it down.

- You're not good enough? Write it down.

- Your feelings of worthlessness? Write it down.

- Your poverty? Write it down

- Your loveless life? Write it down.

- Your poor health? Write it down.

Now. Hold that piece of paper in your hand. Close your eyes. And express your gratitude for these negative beliefs. Yes, thank them! You cannot release them in anger...they will come back to stick to you like a burr. Release them with gratitude and they will release you.

Now. Once you are finished expressing your thankfulness for all the old beliefs you have written down that no longer serve you, it is time to burn that paper. You can bury it as well. But I prefer to release the smoke of what I no longer need into the universe. It will be transformed into something else…something better.

Then get another piece of paper and write down everything you desire.

I desire love.

I desire joy.

I desire to be debt free — financially and karmically.

I desire to be my best self.

Whatever you desire. Write it down. And then fold up the paper and write one word that comes to you on the outside of the folded paper. One word that represents all that you desire.

Freedom

Ease

Peace

Joy

Love

And let that one word be your mantra for the rest of the year. Place the paper on your altar, under or near a candle, by a sacred object, wherever you feel is most appropriate for this little piece of paper that holds your hope.

I like to do this ceremony at the winter solstice and refer to my mantra at the equinoxes and summer solstice. A reaffirming for me. And the mantra becomes a barometer for all I do that year.

On the winter solstice of 2001, my husband and I came up with a mantra of EASE for the coming year. Everything we did was using the barometer of our 2002 mantra. If we were struggling with a decision, then we were not in ease...so we chose the ease and things just started to flow. That's how we found our current home. With ease, it flowed into our lives. In a way that we could not previously imagine.

EASE. What a great mantra. I suggest it to many of my patients who struggle so in their lives. Let go, and be at Ease.

Your mantra is a seed of energy you plant in your consciousness. Writing down your intentions and referring to them throughout the year is watering and fertilizing that seed so it might grow. Some seeds take a long time to sprout. Some grow into trees that take a long time to fruit. The seed of EASE sprouted into a lovely flower garden at first, but truly it is a deep-rooted plant...for EASE continues some fourteen years later bearing us precious fruit.

May this time find you nurturing your mantra seed. May your life be filled with great joy, with love, with beauty and with blossoms that attract butterflies of hope.

59. RELEASING YOUR OLD STORY

Now more than ever, we are experiencing the growing pains of change. Yet we hang onto the old like a worn-out lifeline.

It is human nature to fear change, yet change is part of life. What makes us sick oftentimes are old habits, old paradigms, old storylines that no longer serve us.

How many of us have lived personal story lines of conflict, abandonment, anger, unworthiness, sadness, apathy, poverty consciousness, victim consciousness and more. The energy of our story often precedes us setting a path for our future. We manifest what we believe.

The time is ripe to release our old story.

The challenge is that many of us are still hanging on to those old story lines as if they were attached like an arm or a leg. What if you let your old story lines go?

Every challenge you may be having right now, stems from a long held story-line that has turned into a conflict that you struggle with to be whole and healthy.

Setting our old story lines free with appreciation for the lessons learned can be difficult if we are unaware of our higher purpose.

What if everything, even the "bad" stuff, is really a lesson in love? Learning to love others, love the earth, but most of all — love ourselves.

Some of you might have read Don Miguel Ruiz's book, The Four Agreements.

- Be impeccable with your word.
  What you think and especially what you say — becomes your reality.

- Don't make assumptions.
  There is ALWAYS a deeper meaning, a lesson to be learned, a reason for everything that happens. Learn to perceive with an open mind and generous heart.

- Always do your best.
  Your best is being your truth, being true to your Self, and choosing Love over Fear.

- Don't take anything personally.
  Some of our old story lines are like family heirlooms. We've been carrying the energy of our ancestors, our family stories — the good, the bad and the ugly.

Time to let go of all that does not serve us.

Your body holds onto the energy of these story lines and manifests dis-ease, aging, injury, fatigue, insomnia.

Time to clear the temple of your being.

Learning to Love yourself erases all that no longer serves.

You have to be willing to love yourself so much that you are willing to love and appreciate all even the despair, anguish, shame, blame, guilt, sadness, feeling of betrayal, victim consciousness, poverty consciousness and feeling of unworthiness—everything and release it to the Light of Love.

Here's an exercise that may help:

1) Write down every story that you keep repeating in your life. Then place it under a heading such as self-sabotage, grief, sadness, poverty-consciousness, apathy, unworthiness etc.

2) In stillness and with love, find in your heart appreciation for the story and the part you played. Release each story, one at a

time, with heartfelt love, back to the Divine Light. Say out loud: "I end this story. It is complete."

3) Then take a deep cleansing breath and say out loud and with absolute belief — I Am Love Say it at least 12 times! See inside of yourself how the release of the old stories are making space in your being for something new and abundantly joyous to be played out in your life.

4) When you are ready, simply choose Love and another storyline one that is abundantly rich in passion, love, light, and joy!

May you be blessed with love and light.

60. DANCING WITH DEATH

On January 6th, 2015 life threw me a curve ball.

I took one look at my mother and knew life was about to change. Mom was sick, really sick. And I know sick.

I've been working in the medical field for over thirty years. I can smell disease, feel tumors, see death. And Mom rarely ever gets sick.

But after flying to Utah to spend Christmas with one of my sisters and then driving from LAX to Big Bear to entertain my youngest sister's family for New Years, Mom was tired. And she's never tired! My mom is the Energizer Bunny! Plus she had a strange rash on her her legs.

So that day, despite being "my worst patient" as she proudly claimed, Mom got up on my exam table so I could check her out.

The rash turned out to be phlebitis and I didn't like what I felt in her stomach. And the abdominal ultrasound confirmed my suspicions.

So I consulted with my collaborating physician and ordered a CT scan and a venous Doppler. Mom's bloodwork didn't look great either.

The next week as I was orchestrating Mom's care, my other sister (there's four of us girls, less than four years apart between me and the youngest with twins in between) texted that she was driving from Northern California to check in on Dad.

My parents have been divorced for twenty-five years but still lived in the same town.

Mom drove up to Ojai to stay and work with me, managing my businesses since 1997. And she insisted on driving the seventy miles back home so we could have our separate lives. A very self-sufficient woman, our mother raised us girls to be strong and independent.

Dad seemed to have the same neurological symptoms he had five years earlier, so I set up an appointment with his neurosurgeon, ordered blood, and an MRI.

Mom had a tendency to focus more on others than herself, so I didn't think she needed to know about Dad yet and she was adamant that I not tell my sisters about her until we knew more.

So the next morning, I'm with Mom at the interventional radiologist getting her liver biopsied while juggling calls from my sister regarding Dad's medical care. When it rains, it pours.

That evening my sisters were giving me a hard time for not getting more involved with Dad.

I went in to check on Mom and she took one look at my face and asked what's wrong?

"Please," I begged her, "let me tell my sisters."

She agreed.

I called a conference call knowing my three sisters would think it was regarding Dad. "This isn't about Dad. It's about Mom."

And then the tears began to flow.

The great weight was lifted for a short time. The next day Mom insisted on going back home to pack. Since her venous Doppler showed no signs of deep vein thrombosis, my collaborating physician and the interventional radiologist agreed that she could go home. I let her go, knowing my sister would stay with her.

But Mom felt fine and sent my sister home!

Sunday morning at 7:15, I got a call from Mom's partner. "Deb, the paramedics are here and they want to speak to you."

I instructed the emergency personnel that Mom was probably having a pulmonary embolism. By the time I got to the ER in her home town, they had brought her back to life three times.
I walked into the emergency room – the same one I volunteered as a candy striper before going to UCLA nursing school in 1981.

There I found my mom intubated, panicking, but very much alive.

I kissed her, tried to orient her, asked the nurse to please sedate her, and consulted with the emergency physicians. Then I texted my sisters. "You need to come now." They all flew in that evening. By then mom was in the ICU.

That was Mom's worse nightmare.

I know nearly dying, being intubated and tied down (yes, they use soft restraints to keep the patients from pulling out their ventilation tube) would be most people's worst nightmare, but being taken to that particular hospital was hers.

256

You see, both her parents died in that hospital.

In December 1982, my beloved grandparents moved from Philadelphia to California to be near their only daughter and granddaughters.

I was just a nursing student at UCLA but when Poppop got off that plane, I knew he was going to die. And he did, three weeks later.

Less than two years later, Nana died in that same hospital.

Mom never ever wanted to go there…but there she was in the ICU, unable to communicate with a tube down her throat and her hands tied down. Have you ever seen anyone yell with their eyes?

Thank goodness for my daughter, an ICU nurse, who knew those machines like the back of her hand. The rest of us nurses…yes, three out of the four daughters…hadn't been practicing in the hospital for years.

Five days after that fatalistic call, Mom was discharged from the hospital into my care.

JANUARY 26TH

I type this listening through a baby monitor as Mom's oxygen concentrator hums and puffs, I truly never expected this.

So much has happened, I can hardly breathe. Finally feeling the enormity of this event.

Yes, it's stage IV adenocarcinoma of undetermined primary...probably small bowel as the pancreatic markers are negative. Definitely not breast, colon, lung. PET scan confirmed – no bone mets, no brain mets, nothing in her chest. But three large tumors in her retroperitoneal cavity and many metastasis to her spleen and liver.

I believe her cancer represents her fears. The first one off her duodenum is FEAR. How fear has ruled her life...it's the mothership that launched the rest...otherwise known as the primary tumor. Then there's one inferior to her pancreas, long and lean...I believe it is REGRET...all the regrets of her life, not doing all the things she wanted to, not forgiving herself or others, especially Dad, and Nana. Then there's a smaller tumor near her aorta...this one is DOUBT. How Mom has doubted herself all these years. Never good enough, educated enough, smart enough, brave enough. Then there's her VULNERABILITY splattered as mets on her spleen. She's always been vulnerable to codependent relationships and being taken advantage of. And last, the liver mets represent her WORRY. How much time spent worrying about everything– money, love, other people's drama.

These five fears must be released to be healed.

FEBRUARY 14th

After more than a month, Steve and I got to get away. Just up to Santa Barbara for two nights. A glorious day in the sun, nearly as hot as summer in mid-February, lounging on a private beach. As I stood in the water communing with the Divine Mother, whales swam by and I could feel their energy... "you know what to do."

We just got the final news when we left. My youngest sister told the twins. I tried to prepare them when I got the PET scan and pathology back, but they needed to hear it from the doctor who frankly said very little except that without treatment, Mom has maybe a few months and with treatment, if she can stand being sick all the time, maybe a little longer, up to two years…but eventually the cancer will become resistant.

Mom has chosen to treat her cancer with cannabis. There's no guarantee, but at least she's not in pain, and has an appetite. She's had problems with nausea, dry heaves and occasional vomiting bile, probably due to pancreatitis and tumor obstructing her bile ducts. She's finally off oxygen as the blood clots in her lungs slowly dissolve. She'll be on blood thinners for at least six months.

My sisters might be more comfortable if Mom chose chemo as her treatment option but it's so hard to see her sick and frankly, Mom has never believed in chemo.

At least they agreed to the cannabis. Living with Mom high has been quite the adventure.

This would be so funny, if it wasn't so sad.

FEBRUARY 28th
A few weeks ago, on one of Mom's good days, we were taking a little walk to the mailbox and she stopped and squeezed my arm.

"You know, my cancer is going to catapult your healing practice into the future you've always dreamed of."

"Thanks, Mom, for the many gifts you have given me."

In sickness and in health, for richer or for poorer, we traversed our soul paths together. Without Mom, Full Circle Family Health would have never been realized. Without Mom, I could have never birthed Genesis Health Products. Without Mom, I would have never founded our charity – Divine Daughters Unite. Mom has always been my biggest cheerleader, breathing hope into my dreams even if she couldn't believe in her own.

Sometimes healing means releasing the old ways of being to make way for the new.

Everything's a gift. Our challenge is to be open to receive the gift of each and every encounter.

MARCH 20th

Right now, Mom is at a beach house in Oxnard with my sisters, giving them time to process the reality of the situation. We're not all on the same page medically. So we had a meeting. Mom said there were three rules: no harsh words, we had to laugh, and ultimately remember that this is her decision. One of my sisters is still struggling with letting Mom go. It's better now that she can witness Mom's decline first hand, yet it's still hard.

After my sisters were finished deciding what was best for Mom, I asked her what she felt was happening. She said she thinks that she hasn't decided whether to stay or go and that's why it seems like the cannabis isn't working, that's why she's still sick.

I told her that I do not believe there is any "thing" we can give her that will cure her cancer. I believe that only she has the power to cure herself. And if she chooses to go, I told her I would help her pass as gracefully as possible.

MAY 8th

Mom is gone.

Not to heaven, not yet. She's in Utah.

After that horrific two weeks in March when Mom finally understood she was dying, she returned to my care. She had lost another ten pounds, was weak, dehydrated, worn out from pain. I got her rehydrated, switched her cannabis from oral to suppositories which controls pain and nausea much better without the psychoactive effects – sometimes I feel like I'm on the set of Breaking Bad as I experiment with the best way to formulate cannabis for her.

I called hospice for palliative care, got physical therapy started, and got her to work with a psychospiritual therapist. I then sat down and had a come to Jesus talk with her (or come to Buddha talk, as she was reading Buddhist books at the time). I asked her again if she was ready to die and she said emphatically, NO!

"Then, Mom, you are going to have to take control of your health care. Just like I teach my patients. You must be in the driver's seat when it comes to your health."

Mom showed her true spirit and rallied. She took over her own meds, even learned to administer her own suppositories. Mom was sure she couldn't possibly reach. I reminded her she'd wiping her own but for 70 plus years. She gave me the stink eye, but managed to administer her own suppository. Yes! Goodness knows, if we couldn't find the humor in this cancer-drama and laugh, we'd be crying all the time.

Mom began preparing her own meals and ate every couple of hours trying to gain the pounds she'd lost. She became discouraged when her weight didn't change after a week of trying, so I taught her how to eat consciously. How to not just be grateful for the food, but to bless each and every bite, and instruct that precious food to do for her body what she wished. A week later she had put back on six pounds.

Under the guidance of her therapist, Mom arranged meetings either by phone or in person with the people in her life she needed to release. On Easter Sunday, she even performed a profoundly beautiful and heart wrenching ceremony, first releasing her mother, then my sisters, and finally in tears…me.

I tried to help Mom die consciously, and she began to live consciously.

By mid-April, it was clear Mom had taken a turn for the better. It was time for her to be with my sisters and her other grandchildren. She agreed.

I called my sisters. They were excited that Mom seemed better. I warned them that it was the calm before the storm. The time when the terminally ill rally, seem so much better, then slip away. They didn't care. They just wanted to spend what good days Mom may have left with her.

So I did for Mom what she did for me and released her.

My sister flew out from Utah and drove our mother north. Mom finally got to see Jarys' new apartment and bring him a fruit bowl (because it's not a home unless you have a bowl full of fruit to offer your guests). Then they headed to Vallejo to stay at at the twin's beach house for a few days. Last Monday, my sister flew with Mom to Utah.

It was hard letting her go. Trusting that she would be ok without me. Trusting that I would be ok without her.

It wasn't an easy transition. The day my sister arrived here, Mom got off her schedule, skipped a dose of cannabis, became paranoid, insomniac, emotional. Her change in mood appeared to be chemical, but perhaps it was fear.

Too much, too soon, yet there so little time left to complete her "bucket list" (Mom's terminology, not mine). I don't believe in putting all my dreams, wishes, aspirations into a bucket to do "someday".

I believe the time is NOW – to be fully present each and every moment.

Before she left, Mom wanted to see Kyra. When Mom first got out of the hospital, she dreamt Kyra told her she was having a baby. That evening Kyra gave her a stuffed elephant she bedazzled with her crocheted wedding doilies. She told her Grandma Honey to please sleep with the toy to imprint it with her energy so when she's through with it, Kyra can give the elephant to her babies. After sleeping with it for the past four months, Mom returned the elephant to Kyra.

Mom, Kyra and me, Mother's Day, 2008

At this point I truly wished I felt more confident about this path I'm on with Mom. It was easier when she was here. I could take her pulse and reassure myself that all was well.

She's been gone two weeks and I haven't heard from her. She's in transition from my care to theirs, but since we began working together at Full Circle Family Health, not a week had passed that I hadn't heard Mom's voice, received a text, an email, a Facebook post – something.

Guess I'm being prepared for the inevitable. It's easy to talk. The walk is much, much harder.

One sunny afternoon in late March we were out in the courtyard, enjoying family, food, and music, so I invited Mom to dance. She has always been an amazing dancer. She even danced on American Bandstand in the fifties. Some of my earliest memories are dancing in the living room with my *mother, my baby sisters doing their best to keep up.*

Fifty years later, I held my mother in my arms and we danced. Even through a wave of nausea that day, she kept dancing. Not even cancer could keep her from feeling the music. Mom's the one who taught me that life is a dance. And I now see that the dance never really ends.

JULY 13th

The time has come to say goodbye. Mom is near the end. Like a shooting star whose light is ever so bright, Mom burnt through our lives and our hearts.

Helping her pack in April for her trip to visit my sisters, I found a box shoved under the guest bed. In the poor light, I thought it read "Maria's Dude Box". Mom laughed, "that's my dead box!"

In 2005, Mom joined the Neptune Society. Thank goodness she opted for the travel plan, since she became a gypsy in her last few months.

After a month in Utah, Mom finally landed in Texas. She will take her final breath in my youngest sister's beautiful home. After setting up in-home hospice, I write this on the plane from Houston, coming back to mail out Mom's box. Then I'll return to help release her so she can pass in peace.

The first few weeks after she left, we had no contact. I missed her terribly. She did not answer my calls releasing me perhaps. So I spent my time searching the Internet for clips of her dancing on American Bandstand. And I found her.

In 2002 I was invited as endocrine advisor for Great Smokies Labs (now known as Genova) to review a new cell metabolism test. Everyone else brought their spouses to the lavish dinner aboard the Queen Mary. I brought Mom.

The CEO asked me to help the group of West Coast doctors understand how the new test could be used in our clinical practice. While I was in the midst of my explanation, the CEO could not keep his eyes off Mom. Suddenly, he pointed at her and exclaimed.

"You're Maria from American Bandstand! I rushed home every day after school to watch you dance!"

I searched through several Bandstand clips before I saw my mom's signature dance move. I replayed it over and over. Yep! That's my Mom! Steve thought so too, but just to be sure, I showed it to Mom.

Sitting on my sister's couch next to Mom, we watched the clip. She immediately started naming the dancers including her cousin and friend. And of course, herself. Watching my sister's face the moment she recognized Mom was precious.

Mom told me that my grandparents didn't approve of her going to North Philly. It was rough. After school, they took a bus from South Philly, then a monorail train, and waited with the "regs" at Pops soda shop to be called on stage. Mom said the "good dancers" always got called with the "regs" (the regular bandstand dancers). Of course, she always got called.

She acts like it was nothing. "I was embarrassed when that CEO recognized me. He became a doctor and my claim to fame is a dancer on American Bandstand!"

Not your only claim to fame, Mom. No, there are thousands of Full Circle Family Health patients who will never forget how you made them feel like family. There are hundreds of people who you served and cared for in your community. There are dozens of young women you taught as a Girl Scout leader. There are nine grandchildren, two great grandchildren, three grand son-in-laws, one granddaughter-in-law to be, three son-in-laws, and three other daughters who you loved and mothered fiercely, passionately, thoroughly.

And there's me, your eldest daughter. I could have never become the nurse practitioner, the mother, the wife, the friend, the woman I am without you teaching me how to dance through all of life's transitions.

Especially this, our last dance on earth.

It's hard to let your loved one go. My youngest sister an RN was quite capable of starting hospice. She just needed permission. She needed me to say it's time. The twins, still struggling in denial of the fact that our mother is dying, were encouraging her to do more. But neither of us nurse practitioner sisters were there when Mom started going downhill. I told my youngest sister that I trusted her to be our eyes, our ears, our hands. I trusted her nursing instinct. And she was right. Mom's liver is failing now.

Both my youngest sister and I married our high school sweethearts. Before Mom got sick, my sister and her husband booked a 30th anniversary trip to Italy. Mom insists that they go. "Don't change your whole life for me!" My sister's afraid to go and leave Mom with the non-medical twin, the one most afraid of death. So I'm flying back to Houston on Friday and I'll stay until my sister returns eleven days later. She thanked me for making her feel safe. I hope I can help the twins make peace with this. Mom hopes so too.

And Mom promised to wait for me.

I am forever grateful for the past 17 years I was able to work side by side with Mom. We laughed, we cried, we argued, we hugged. We always kissed so long. Never goodbye.

No matter how many miles away she is, I feel her. I don't believe this will change when she releases her body. Mom will always be with me, always a part of me.

I spent Sunday afternoon calling all the relatives. Mom hasn't been able to answer their calls for a couple of weeks now. Her best friend and her cousin bemoaned not coming to see her. "But you did see her. When she was well last year." Mom was divinely guided. She went back to Philly last summer and had a great time with her childhood friends and cousins. If she knew it was "good bye", she might not have been as free to enjoy the precious moment of Now.

Unfortunately, Mom's not ready. Her body is done, but her spirit is strong. She wanted to hold another great-grandbaby. The hospice chaplain reassured her that she will, before anyone else. She will hold each and every one of the babies to come.

I pray to be able to help her be at peace.

Just as she birthed me into this world, I am privileged to midwife her into the spirit world.

Life is sweet and sweeter yet when you're dancing with death. And we're enjoying every step with Mom!

Death is not an ending; it's a beginning of a new way of being.

JULY 22nd

I arrived in Houston Friday night under a crescent moon just like when I was born. Mom birthed me into this world and now I was there to help birth her into the spirit world.

I am Mom's doula...holding vigil as she dies. I've dreamt it. Me, Jarys, Kyra forming the triad necessary to hold open the portal.

I've been dreaming of Mom a lot, mostly me taking care of her and she's a little girl, sometimes a baby. A couple of weeks ago, I had a dream that she looked like one of those troll dolls I used to play with when I was a kid. You know the kind – stick up hair, small carved face, pot belly and impossibly big feet.

When I saw her the first time I came to Houston, gosh, that was just a week ago, Mom looked just like she did in my dream. The edema made her feet look impossibly big; the cancer swelled her belly to the size of an eight month pregnancy and consumed the rest of her flesh so her upper body was tiny and her teeth seemed too big for her face. To complete the image, my sister had colored her hair the same reddish brown I saw in my dreams and it was sticking straight up.

Saturday Mom rallied. She woke up hungry after her big dose of bedtime cannabis. She had a dip egg and toast, some watermelon and then a nap. I fed her three times, got her up to the bedside commode, but her kidneys were shutting down. It'd be soon.

My sister and her husband left for their anniversary trip to Italy. Mom asked for a malocchio from the motherland. She won't be here when they get back.

274

My sister had been holding off giving Mom opiates, using the cannabis for the pain, trying to keep her lucid for me and the twins. As soon as they got to the airport, the pain became so intense I had to start the opiates. The first dose knocked her out for twelve hours. So far out, I had to give her oxygen to keep her lucid for my other sister to arrive. And hopefully for my children. They were due to arrive on Monday.

She waited for my sister to leave to begin the process of dying.

She waited for me to midwife her death.

Sunday morning I got Mom up for the last time to the commode but for naught. Her kidneys had shut down. But with the help of my nephew's fiancé, I gave my Mom a spit bath on the commode. Gotta meet death looking your best.

Dying is very much like giving birth. There's the burst of energy, then the labor begins. For Mom birthing us was difficult. Dying wasn't easy. The labor began on Sunday.

So I created an altar for Mom. One devoted to her peaceful release. She's blessed to be here, to have her daughters and grandchildren rally around her. This process of dying is hard on those unused to witnessing the end. I've done it many times. As a nurse, my daughter is used to it too. My youngest sister witnessed the demise of both of her in laws. And it was quite traumatic hospital experiences. As much as I hoped Mom would come home to California so I could help her through this portal, I believe she came here as a gift for my sister and her boys. To witness a peaceful passing filled with love.

Mom's hospital bed was placed near big bright windows where she could look out at my sister's beautiful pool and fountains, see the kids swim and play. We congregated in the great room with Mom. Singing to her, massaging her limbs, kissing her cheeks, bugging her I'm sure, but heck, it's our Italian way to love you to death.

After I anointed Mom then did some energy work to help her release her form, she seemed to leave her body. There would periods of peaceful sleep, then she would be slammed back into her painful dying body. She would thrash about restlessly and moan in agony.

I had to begin the drugs given to us by hospice to relieve her pain, trying to give her the least amount possible to keep her comfortable but lucid for when my other sister arrived.

A few hours after I did the release work, both my husband at home and my sister in Italy texted me: Did Mom pass yet?

When I replied: No, she's still with us, they were surprised. They both felt like she was with them. So Mom really was out of her body that day, perusing the ethers.

I read her "Death as a Birth" from <u>LoveDance</u>® – the chapter in which Yeshua helps Mary's grandmother die. When I wrote it eleven years ago, I was more like Mary very much attached to the form, but now I feel more like Yeshua, knowing that this body does not contain us.

"Love is eternal and since each of us is Love, then we are also eternal. Not the body. No, the body will die. But who I am as Love can never die. I have always been Love and so have you."

Yeshua begins by teaching the children how death is a birth into the spirit world. And the chapter ends with the children celebrating their great-grandmother's death with a birthday party.

When my sister finally arrived that night, Mom seemed to recognize her then really perked up when my sister played an audio of the great-grandchildren singing: "Happy Birthday to Grandma Honey." I guess she was listening.

Monday was the hardest day. My kids missed their connecting flight and didn't arrive until after midnight. It was all we could do to keep Mom with us. When they got off the plane, I had Jarys call to keep her going. He ran through the airport singing "Ah Maria" the same Louis Prima song my grandfather sang to Mom when she was little.

As soon as they arrived, my daughter quietly stepped in, explaining to her sibling what was going on, her aunt and cousin listening intently. I felt such a great relief to share the medical aspect of death with Kyra. Finally, I could be with my mother as her daughter.

Kyra decided we should make a giant bed to be closer to Grandma Honey. So the boys pulled the ottoman, love seat and chair up against the bed to create a playpen. My children and I climbed in with her. Our intimacy with death, frightened my sister and nephew, but in the end they joined us.

Mom's transition was actually quite beautiful. My daughter and I laid on each side of her, holding her in our arms while my son prayed and sang "Ah, Maria". I witnessed her last breath, heard her last heartbeat. Her soul just floated peacefully out.

On July 21st at 3:33 am PST, Maria Anna Diodato returned to the spirit world.

I called my sister in Italy. She cried and told me that while she planned to get the malocchio on Mary Magdalen's feast day on the 22nd, Mom had come to her and said "you'd better get it now". I called her five minutes after she purchased the malocchio.

The business of death took over the rest of the day. I handled hospice, the Neptune Society, called all the relatives on the East and the West Coast and stayed up when the rest of the family passed out from exhaustion to talk to a couple of patients. Mom never got the chance to use her bell to keep me on schedule like she used to in the office.

After hospice left, we let the dog back in the house. My sister's chocolate lab had held vigil with me the entire time. She laid by Mom's bed day and night. She came in wagging her tail, went to her toy basket, and then to Mom's bed, where she gently placed her purple ball, then walked quietly away. A gift for the afterlife. By the end of the day, after holding it together to deal with everyone else's grief, I fell into a dreamless sleep. We spent the next couple of days sharing Grandma Honey stories, eating her favorite foods. I changed my flight to leave early with the kids knowing I could not truly grieve until I was home in Steve's arms.

When I arrived in Ojai, Mom's energy greeted me. She's permeated every aspect of the office. I can hear her footsteps coming down the hall as she calls for me. I laid on the lounge under the oak tree where she spent time recovering from her hospitalization.

There's a Native American saying: "The soul would have no rainbows, if the eyes had no tears."

My soul is very colorful right now.

I am blessed to have been able to share my home, my life, my children, my dreams with Mom. She helped me accomplish my vision of an integrative health practice and then ran all three of my businesses for eighteen years. She helped me found Divine

Daughters Unite, a nonprofit organization that empowers young women through charitable works. She was the eldest board member.

Since Mom passed, there's been an empty space behind me. She liked to come up behind me, wrap her arms around me and kiss my neck. I shared this with my sister in Italy. A few minutes later, Kyra said her aunt texted her that I needed a "Grandma hug" and gave me one. So sweet, yet it's always been Mom who had my back.

Still she must be busy. We've been trying to get a business credit line for the last four years. This past month, I've been getting lots of offers for funding in the mail, some with deadlines due soon. So before I left for Houston, I connected with Mom and intuitively chose one, applied over the phone, and forgot about it.

The day after she died, I got a call. It was from the bank. "Congratulations, you got the credit line!"

I cried, "Thank you, Mom."

The bank rep was confused, "My name is Todd."

"I'm thanking my mother, Todd. She's pulling some strings in heaven as we speak!"

It's surreal living without her.

I'm not sure how to be a motherless daughter.

I know she's with me in spirit, but I sure miss her hugs.

Thank you, Mom, for dancing with me all of my life and now in spirit form.

AUGUST 6TH
Where is Mom but within me?

I feel her when I think of my sisters and how hard they are trying in their own lives. About their soul lessons and wishing them the best of luck and enlightenment. It's strange. Losing mother yet gaining her as an aspect of self.

I had a dream that illustrates my view of the circle of life and death.

I am on a great stage with all my family, my sisters, my children, my friends, my patients. Everyone I know and love are there on stage with me acting out their parts in this play called Life. And there is a thick, thick curtain separating the backstage from the front. Most of the other actors in the play do not seem to know what's backstage or who's directing us. I know Mom is backstage, with all my dead loved ones, preparing me, guiding me. I know where the curtain parts and slip between to be with her. And I can also see from the director's view - this great play, both on stage and backstage - everything connected. I feel comforted by this connectedness and wake up smiling.

For Mom, the pain and the joy could not be mixed. Family and friends were her joy. Cancer sucks. Like all dis-ease, I believe it is symbolic of buried emotions hiding deep soul issues. During the last months of Mom's life, she released a lot of pent up painful emotions. While she was with me, I tried to escort her to those dark places to release the karmic suffering that inevitably gets passed on to your children and grandchildren.

My journey with Mom. So much insight. So much spiritual healing. As much as she could, Mom allowed me to disentangle the family cords that bind us in guilt, shame, disappointment and fear. This spiritual work was a great part of our work together for the past 13 years. It wasn't just healing others, it was healing ourselves.

Through this heart-wrenching journey with Mom, I was set free and now so are my children. She is so very present for me, more so than when she was alive. Since I was a tiny child, I could sense her emotions, her pain, her fear. I could call her to me when we were miles apart, just like I did with Nana. I was so fortunate that she was open enough to respond. So many stories, most have no idea how gifted Mom was and is.

On the blue moon, just ten days after her death, she showed me in a meditation that fear (in all its forms -guilt, shame, anger, disappointment) is like a thick bank of fog that is so very difficult for her to penetrate. She comes easily to me (rather through me as it feels like she is part of me now) because I released my fear.

Oh yes, I had guilt about not being able to save her. My first dream of her after she died was a guilt dream. Since then she has come through me sharing precious wisdom, like my left breast pain which used to be her "boob alert" - meaning something was wrong in the family- I have it now. She told me it's my sense of responsibility for everyone and to LET IT GO! I'm working on it.

We grieve what we've lost, what will never be. Yet life goes on or rather Love. Love goes on.

Mom was Love pure and simple. I feel her in me...the way she loved me, my sisters, my nieces and nephews, even my husband who she loved like a son. The quality of my feelings towards my family, especially my sisters, have shifted since she died. I truly Feel Her. I Feel the Way She Feels about them. It's rather amazing. I have more maternal compassion than ever before. I even see myself with new eyes - her eyes!

So let's release our fear and remember her laughter, her wisdom, her joy.

That is how our loved ones can be with us, when we're happy!

61. SISTER-BOND

AUGUST 13TH

Just returned from the arms of my adopted grandmother. First time I've been held since Momma passed. The business of death has occupied my mind. My responsibilities to my patients have occupied my time. More family health dramas have occupied my heart. There is little room for grieving.

As I sit waiting for my beloved to recover from surgery, I ponder the words of my wise friend. "In the wake of your mother's death, your spousal concerns shall bring you closer together." Then I hear the wedding vows we each made...

"In sickness and in health. For richer or for poorer. Till death do us part...Or in the case of my marriage to Steve - until the end of time...

And I think how these same vows were made before birth. To our sisters. We may disagree, yet never fall out of love. We may move thousands of miles apart, yet our bonds are never broken. We may dance to different drummers, yet forever appreciate our uniqueness. Through sickness and in health. For richer or for poorer. Till death do us part. Our sisters, both blood and soul, have always been there, will always be there.

All our drama over the years becomes refined into blessed life lessons. Every one experienced differently, yet lessons all the same. Some grow right away, some take the course again and again, until each of us are a more refined version of ourselves.

286

Sisters never fail you. They rejoice with you. They grieve with you. They tell you the awful truth and love you even when you are not ready to receive it. They wait for you to figure out life and delight in your growth. They pray for you. They believe in you.

And when you've fallen to your greatest depths of despair, they are there to pick you up, brush you off, help you put on your big girl panties, fix your makeup, and face the world.

Momma always wished she had sisters. It broke her heart when we didn't get along. It brought her so much joy when we embraced each other. We thought Mom was the bridge between us, yet her death has shown us that she stitched us together so tightly that our hearts beat as one.

I love you, dear sisters, more than you know.

My 50th birthday celebration with Mom and my sisters.

62. BECOMING THE MATRIARCH

In January, I realized Mom was dying.

In July, she died in my arms.

The first half of 2015 forged my soul in the most transformative fire.

The second half tested my spiritual steel through the flames of change.

Karmic hell broke loose when Mom passed through the veils of heaven.

All of our husbands immediately faced a major health hurdle.

One is still fighting for his life.

Our father had emergency brain surgery.

All nine grandchildren had to grow up fast.

For the first time my sisters and I turned to each other for spiritual support.

There was no one else who truly understood our pain.

The moment Mom took her last breath, I became the matriarch of the family.

I should have known this was coming. I was warned just two months before.

On the Big Island of Hawaii on the Day of the Dead 2014, I dreamt of Nana.

A lava petroglyph wall towers before me. I float up the wall and go through it into a doorway which leads to a light room - the kitchen from my infancy.

My deceased aunt greets me fussing around a pink Formica table where Nana sits. Nana is the queen bee. My aunt says they cannot make much here. I tell them not to worry, I will get them whatever they need and they can make whatever they want.

Nana shows me that they are limited in their heavenly experience to what they chose to experience in life on earth. She is surprised I am there, yet also expected me. I hug her and she feels so real. I wonder why she appears as I remember her in her fifties and not as a young woman. She shows me that her afterlife appearance is that of her at the prime of her power in the life I knew her.

Nana places a shawl over my shoulders. It's the matriarchal mantle. I wonder how with Mom still here.

Nana kisses my forehead and whispers "It's your turn to lead"...

290

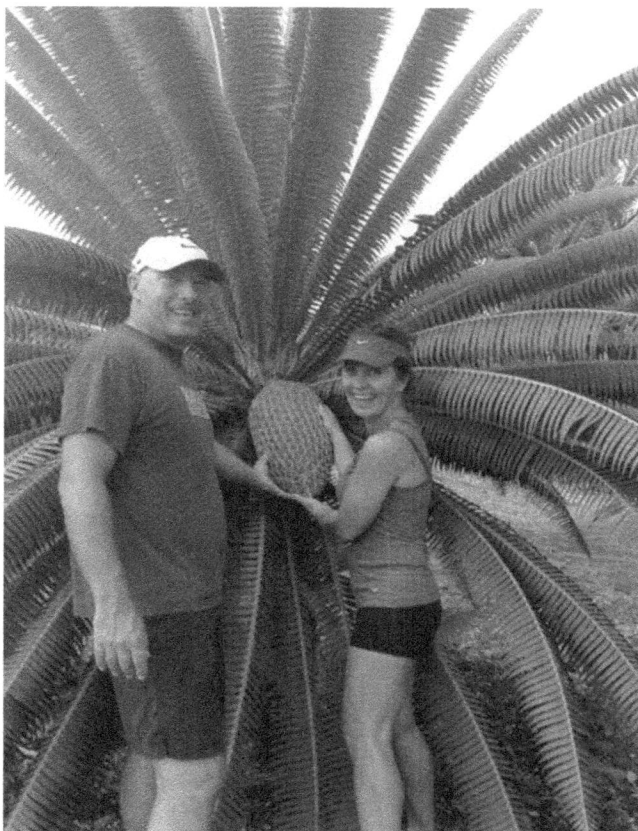
Hawaii, 2014

Every November I set my intentions for the next business year. I would gather all the numbers from Mom who ran all three of my corporations – Full Circle Family Health, Genesis Health Products, and my charity Divine Daughters Unite. She would remind me that the holidays were traditionally slow. But after returning from Hawaii, I took the bull by the horns and tried to figure out why I wasn't more successful.

Granted I had a successful marriage, beautiful healthy children, great relationships with my parents, my siblings, my friends and there was always just enough to meet our needs, yet...I had planned to be able to retire with my husband. And there was never enough to save for that future.

I meditated on why money did not flow with ease... And I heard loud and clear.

"It's me. I'm blocking the flow!"

I fell asleep that night asking to be shown how to get out of my own way.

The next morning three emails landed in my inbox.

The first was a digital course on how to use YouTube to increase your business.

The second was an invitation to join a mastermind for integrative health practitioners who wanted to increase their cash flow.

These third was a webinar on how to release blockages regarding wealth, health, and relationships.

I signed up for all three.

I got my one and only video up and optimized on YouTube and forgot about it.

The mastermind for integrative health practitioners started in January. Once Mom got sick, I realized I wouldn't be able to implement what I was learning. Trying to get vital financial information from my high, hypoxic mother was difficult. Thank goodness, Steve was retired. He helped me take care of Mom while I tried desperately to save my businesses.

The leader of the mastermind took pity on me and offered to help me figure out my business finances. Thank goodness!

But it was releasing the money block that allowed me to thrive during this crisis.

I was reminded during that webinar about the crucial brain wave states of childhood. From two to six years old we are in a theta brain wave state. The same brain waves as meditation and hypnosis. Highly suggestible. We are imprinted at a very young age and function from these limiting subconscious beliefs.

So I did a regression on myself. I got into a theta wave state by meditating with the intention to "see" myself at the age of two. And I was transported to the backseat of a 1958 sedan, sitting between my godmother and my twin baby sisters' car bed. Mommy and Daddy were in the front seat. We were driving to California and in the pit of my tummy, I could feel a pulling sensation as if I was being torn away from my Nana back in Philadelphia.

The next scene, I'm in a toddler bed in the hallway of our new apartment in Burbank, sucking my thumb. I feel all alone and scared that there is no Nana here. And realize that I have to be the Nana now.

Disturbed by the emotion of this regression, I bring myself back. *What did that have to do with my money block?* I shared my vision with Mom and she confirmed it all, down to my bed in the hall since there was no room for me in the one bedroom with their double bed and the two cribs.

Before going to sleep that night, I wrote on a slip of paper: Show me what my regression had to do with money.

And I have a dream.

I'm back in the backseat of the old sedan. This time I'm an adult holding my two-year-old niece in my lap. Her mother hands her a churro. Before the baby starts to put the sticky treat in her mouth, I peel back the paper…it's wrapped in dollar bills!

"No, baby, money's dirty!"

And I wake up shaking from head to toe. I told Mom the dream and she said "Oh, no, money's dirty, Nana said that to you all the time!"

That was my subconscious limiting belief!

No wonder I had trouble handling money, never kept cash on me, let Steve handle the household bills, and Mom handle the business finances. Money's dirty!

Plus in my mother's family, money really was dirty. Poppop was a bookie for the mafia. So much energy of dirty money.

So just before the holidays, I spent time reprogramming myself. I would get into a theta brain wave meditating with theta music.

Then I would repeat this mantra over and over:

"Money's good. Money is power. Power is good."

Why power?

Because I truly believe that what we're really afraid of is our power, so we either misuse it or deny it.

Time to heal my money/power wound.

Thank goodness! For just a few short weeks later, I had to face my biggest fear. Handling all the money by myself. And I did it.

In fact, in spite of taking so much time off to take care of Mom, doing virtually no online marketing, having to hire new staff, new accountants, new bookkeepers, investing in new software to become more automated, in spite of all my fears, my businesses did better in 2015 than any other year previously.

The financial advice helped me take the reins of my business.

My video on YouTube did the advertising for me.

Yet it was the release of my subconscious limiting belief about money that opened me up to receive abundance.

What are subconscious limiting beliefs are keeping you from being your best self?

63. HE ASCENDED, SHE REMAINS

January 18th

Dreamt of Mom. In my dream, I witnessed some animal cruelty and when I broached the subject to my friends and family (all dressed in white upon a stage) they scoffed – why do you care? I said because the Divine is in everything, every creature, every plant, every rock. They turned their backs on me stating – Christ is only with the believers.

I disagreed and went to ask Mom. I found her on the other side of the veil dressed in a long purple robe gathering stuff from my bedside table. I asked her why the others did not perceive Christ consciousness in all? I really thought she could convince them.

She said, "If they don't notice me, (indicating dead loved ones, angels, and spirit guides), how can you expect them to notice HER?"

She handed me an armful of stuff and motioned for me to follow her, saying: "SHE is everywhere, able to intimately connect with each and every one, yet only those in deep prayer may feel HER and they think it's HIM. It's HER Presence, not HIS Essence, that they perceive."

She is the wind, the earth, the waters
She is fire and its heat
She is snow and its cold
She is bird song, butterfly wings, lion's roar, raindrops
She is baby's breath, lovers' embrace, a full belly
She is joy, love, abundance
She is you
She is ageless, timeless, formless
She is solid as rock, fine as dust
She is presence, never judgement
She is the ear of God, the portal to your divinity
He ascended, She remains

"She's born again in you, my daughter. We've always known. They all see it. It frightens them because… You have kept her under wraps, afraid to be your truth. You wrote in a Her voice. She awakened you to Your Divinity and came alive in you." (Mom referred to LoveDance®: Awakening the Divine Daughter)

Mom said, "I feared it. I was afraid for you to be Her. Perhaps you still feel my fear to go out in the world with Her power. Well, that draws to you the disbelievers, the ones more open may resent your interference just stepping into their lives even though they invited you."

"The beautiful wise horas. Ageless, timeless, limitless. That is who you are.

"You are She. Shekhina. The Presence of the Divine.

"Don't be sad they don't see you. They don't see me. They don't see Her.

"Place your hands on what you wish to heal and it will be.

"Imagine your world and it will be.

"Cast off fear, doubt, controversy of any kind. Those are garments of old that no longer suit you. Wear yourself with pride, assuredly. Love them where they are.

"55 is a magical year. Magic is afoot. Everything will change for you. No more struggle. No more fear. You are safe in Her arms. She is invincible and always You."

All will be well.

I have a sense of peace that I didn't have before.

64. BE THE CALM IN YOUR LIFE

Life is stressful. So many pressures on you. From work. Family. Friends. Perhaps you're worried about things beyond your control. No matter what life serves you, it's how you react that creates the rhythm of your existence.

After returning from a business trip in Canada, my husband and I decided to celebrate with the nice wine I brought home and local fresh oysters. I was preparing the salad while he shucked the oysters out by the barbecue.

"Uh, oh. This isn't good." And next thing I know he's standing at the kitchen door bleeding profusely.

I quickly assessed his injury, determined he's severed an artery, and applied pressure. Drove him to the emergency room and set up an appointment with a hand surgeon to repair his tendon.

When we returned home, my husband says, "I really appreciate how calm you always are during an emergency."

I shrugged it off. As a health care provider, I'm well trained. He shook his head, "I was a cop for thirty years and I was trained to be calm while at work, but at home, watching your loved ones in pain, in danger, well, it's hard to be calm."

That got me thinking, how do I stay calm in the face of major stressors?

It seems innate. I remember being calm as a child when havoc would break out at home. It's like I was in a bubble of peace.

Then I realized that being CALM was a conscious choice I make every time I face chaos.

So here it is: My formula for Being the CALM in Your Life. CALM stands for:

C - Connect

A - Attitude

L - Love

M – Meditation

Connect

First, I connect with my breath.

Taking a deep conscious breath allows me to center myself, brings oxygen into every cell so I can think clearly and act decisively, connects me to my higher power, inner strength, divine wisdom, whatever you call it— I become my own best guru!

So when facing a stressful situation, stop and take a deep breath.

I like to hold my hands down in a V at my lap and breathe all the way to my finger tips, filling my lungs with oxygen. Then slowly, consciously exhale out all my fear, all that doesn't serve me.

Sometimes it takes three of these deep conscious breaths to really let go of my fear and CONNECT to my strength.

Attitude

Your attitude is everything. It directs how you will react to a situation. You can either see the stressful situation as an Opportunity or an Obstacle. The choice is yours.

Switching your attitude from negative to positive is as simple as choosing to see it as an opportunity to learn, to grow, to change.

Love

Love and fear are on the opposite ends of the spectrum of emotion. Just like darkness is the absence of light, fear is the absence of love.
Choosing to perceive every situation through the eyes of love will ultimately bring you joy.

Choosing to perceive life through the lens of fear will bring you more pain, more fear.

After taking a deep breath, seeing the opportunity in the stressful situation, choosing love over fear, I say to myself:

"May I be open to receive the gift of this encounter."

And I always do. Receive the gift, that is!

Meditation

Meditating daily even just for a few minutes helps seal CALM into yourself.

Start by finding a quiet place to sit. Get comfortable.

Bring your hands up in prayer position then let them drop fingertips down in a V in your lap. Notice how much more relaxed your shoulders are in this position.

Practice breathing deeply. Once to the center of your chest.

Exhale out all the negative feelings.

Second breath is to your solar plexus where your ribs meet above your belly. Exhale out all that doesn't serve your highest good. Third breath is all the way to the V of your fingertips on your lap.

Of course, your lungs cannot fill up all the way to your pelvis, but focusing on breathing that deeply engages your stomach muscles so that you get the most air. Hold it for a second or so and then slowly exhale. This time breathe out Love!

Now that you're filled with oxygen, you will notice a deep relaxation spread through your body.

See a stressful situation you are facing not as an obstacle, but as an opportunity. Hold the image of the opportunity that just might come from the stress in your mind's eye. You don't need to imagine all the good that will come from this wrinkle in the road of life yet, just be open.

While you are breathing quietly, imagine something or someone you really love. Now look at your stressor with those same eyes of love. Love colors everything brighter.

Repeat this mantra at least ten times

May I be open to receive the gift of this encounter.

Practice this meditation when you arise and before you fall asleep. If the day has been extra stressful, review it through this meditation. Breathe consciously, shift your Attitude, choose Love and relook at the stressor. You may then be able to receive the gift of the encounter.

A few minutes of meditation every day will allow your reaction to life stressors to be CALM.

Using Scent and Sound to be Calm

Another way to train your body to calm down quickly is to meditate with scent and sound.

Using a soothing scent like lavender, chamomile, or vanilla can also help calm your nervous system.

Try essential oils, hydrolyzed sprays, even scented candles. Using the same soothing scent every time you meditate will train your body to associate the scent with calmness.

You can then carry the scent in the form of a spray or essential oil to use in a stressful situation and you will calm down immediately.

Playing soothing music while meditating can help lower your stress hormones.

As you practice meditating to your peaceful music, your body relaxes, your blood pressure and heart rate lowers, your breathing deepens, and you produce less stress hormones and more calming neurotransmitters.

Pick a tune that you can easily hum. That way in the face of a stressful event, you can begin humming the tune and your body will immediately go into a calm meditative state.

Now You can be the Calm in your Life!

65. REMEMBRANCE OF LOVE

Hmm. I didn't think I was done writing my story…for the story goes on…when do you finish?

Yet it feels like it's time to wrap this up. There will be more. I am not through living and learning on this glorious earth. There is much I want to do. Especially share what I know with the world. One of my dreams is to mentor my colleagues and now, I believe, finally the time is ripe.

Yet I present my story to you first. Why?

Because you are the ones who are demanding the change. You want transformation in your lives. You desire integration in everything — your family and working life, your spiritual and worldly life, your health care both alternative and conventional.

Why not blend the science of medicine with the art of healing?

It's what I've been doing as a family nurse practitioner using Intuitive Integrative Medicine since the Harmonic Convergence in 1987. An auspicious time to create change. To transform self and old paradigms.

I have been trying to teach my colleagues for a very long time…few have the courage to bridge the mind-body medicine let alone heal souls. Yet it is time to be whole. Time for my medical colleagues to treat the whole person and teach them how to heal. But first the doctors must heal themselves.

In the summer of 2007, I gave an Intuitive Integrative Medicine workshop. Forty physicians, nurse practitioners, chiropractors, and naturopaths gathered at beautiful Lake Tahoe in California. In the mist of the serene mountains with the audience open to receive my message, I shared my pearls of healing wisdom.

After ending the workshop with a lesson from LoveDance® (how to disentangle our cords of attachment), one young doctor clutched the book to his chest and said, "If you teach us what you know, then we can be your disciples."

His friend laughed, "Do you even know what her book is about?"

He shook his head, "No, but the cover is so beautiful."

"It's about Mary Magdalen!"

"I said something profound?" He wondered.

Yes, young doctor, you did.

May the council gather once again to heal this dimension — heart and soul.

And may you, my friend, create a wave of change by asking for integration from your health care providers. And then maybe…they will be like that young doctor and wish to practice Intuitive Integrative Health. And we will all wake up to our divine potential to heal ourselves.

66. UNTIL WE MEET AGAIN

Life is about change. Strangers become family. Friends drift into strangers.

Love is a choice.

To face every situation with eyes of beauty, with the voice of compassion, with ears of empathy, with a heart of love is a choice.

But you could choose fear.

The world is chaotic. Life keeps happening.

Fear manifests as worry, anger, disappointment.

Love manifests as hope, joy, acceptance.

It's simple. You train your brain and body to respond in fear or in love.

It's a choice.

So, my friend, may you always choose Love.

Love and Light,

Deborah

ABOUT THE AUTHOR

Deborah Maragopoulos MN FNP blends the Science of Medicine with the Art of Healing. Upon graduating from UCLA with a Masters in Nursing, Deborah studied nutritional science, functional medicine, quantum physics, genetics, neuro-immune-endocrinology, and metaphysical healing. Through two decades of clinical research, Deborah developed a unique intuitive integrative health care model, as well as a promising nutraceutical product — Genesis Gold®. An inspirational speaker, Deborah has shared her pearls of wisdom at the California Women's Expo, the Southern California Women's Herbal Symposium, Samuel Merritt College, and the American College of Nurse Practitioners. President of Genesis Health Products Inc, clinical endocrine advisor to Genova Laboratory and Sansum Medical Clinic, past president of California Association of Nurse Practitioners, advisor for the international Women's Economic Forum and bestselling author, Deborah founded Divine Daughters Unite, a nonprofit with the mission to heal a woman is to heal her family, her village, and her world. Deborah lives with her beloved husband in the healing Ojai Valley.

MY LOVEDANCE

Deborah's other books:

- ❖ LoveDance®- The Awakening of the Divine Daughter

- ❖ Hormones in Harmony®- Heal Your Hypothalamus for Graceful Aging, Vibrant Energy, and Optimal Health

Connect with Deborah: *@thehormonequeen*

- ❖ Facebook
- ❖ Instagram
- ❖ YouTube
- ❖ Twitter

All book sales support the non-profit: Divine Daughters Unite.

www.ingramcontent.com/pod-product-compliance
Lightning Source LLC
Chambersburg PA
CBHW031941080426
42735CB00007B/222